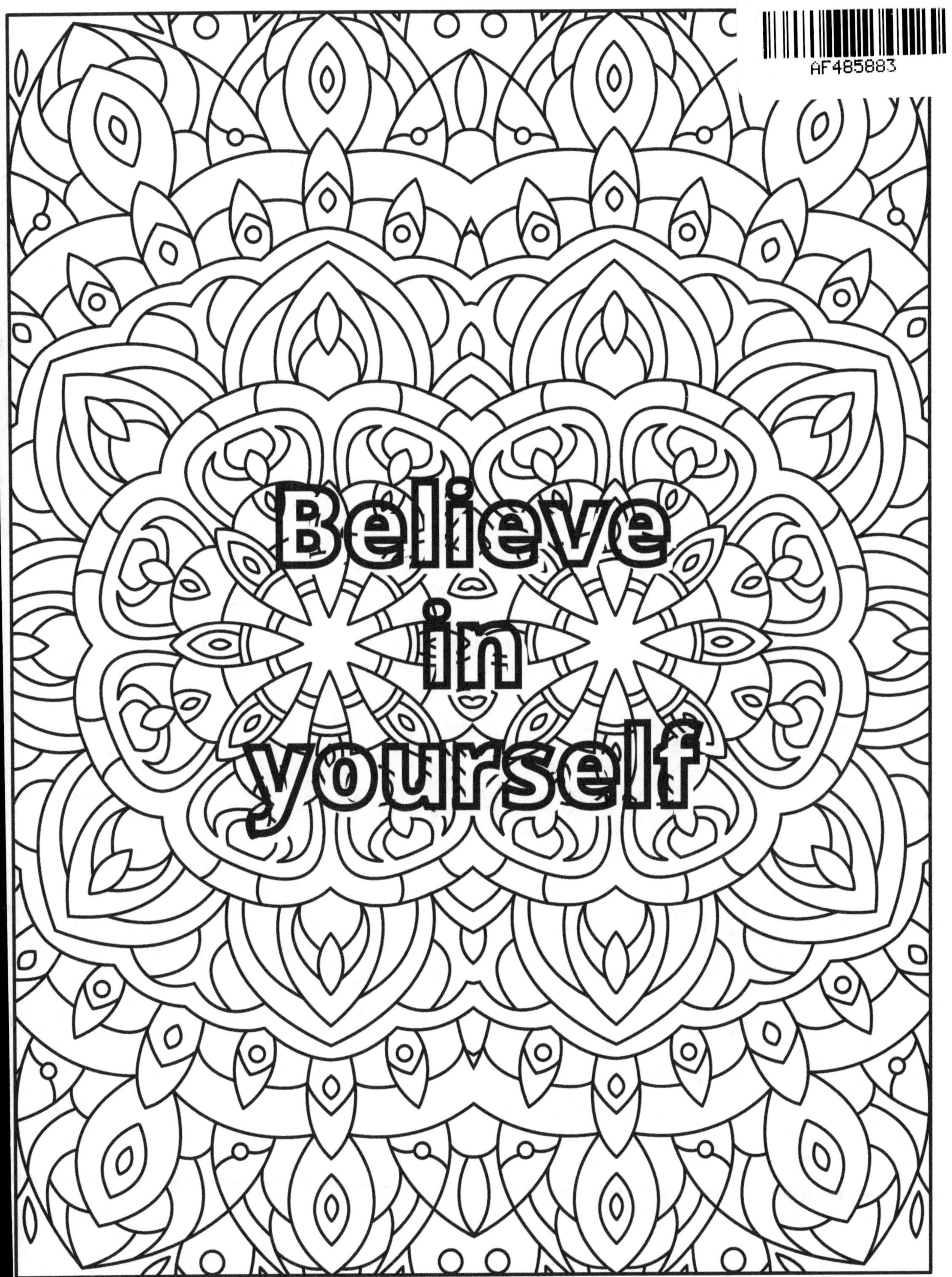
Believe
in
yourself

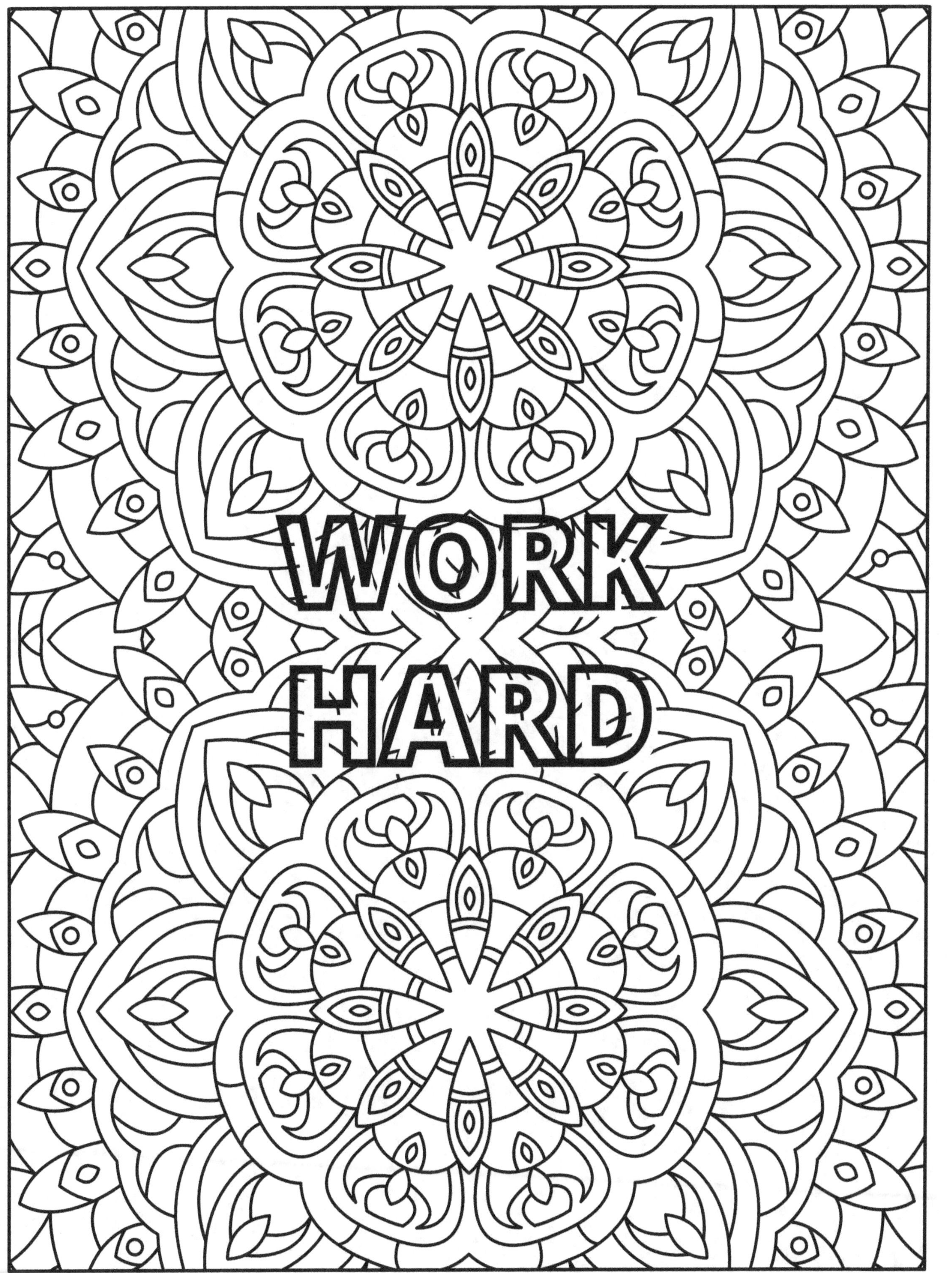

WORK
HARD

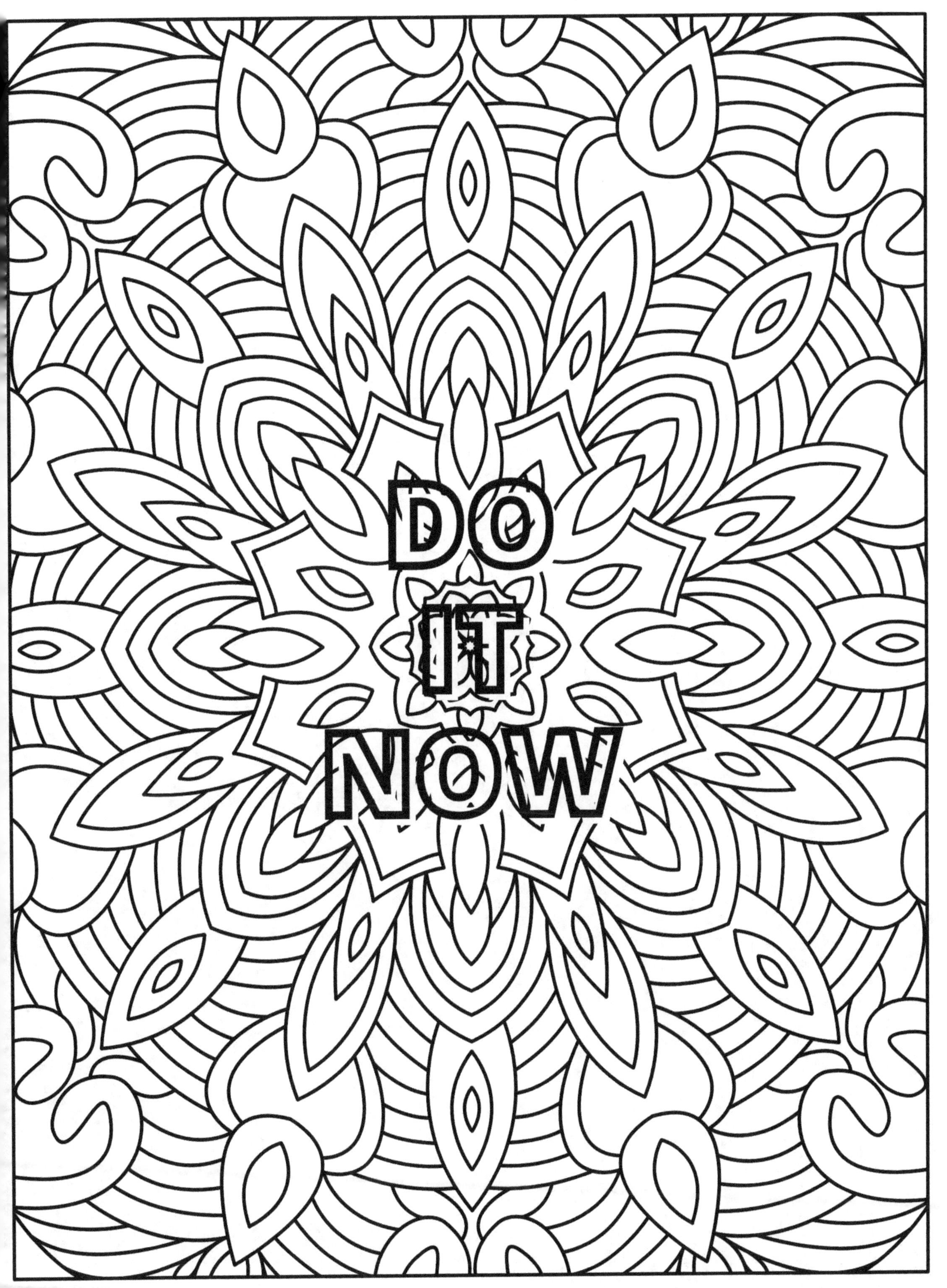

DO
IT
NOW

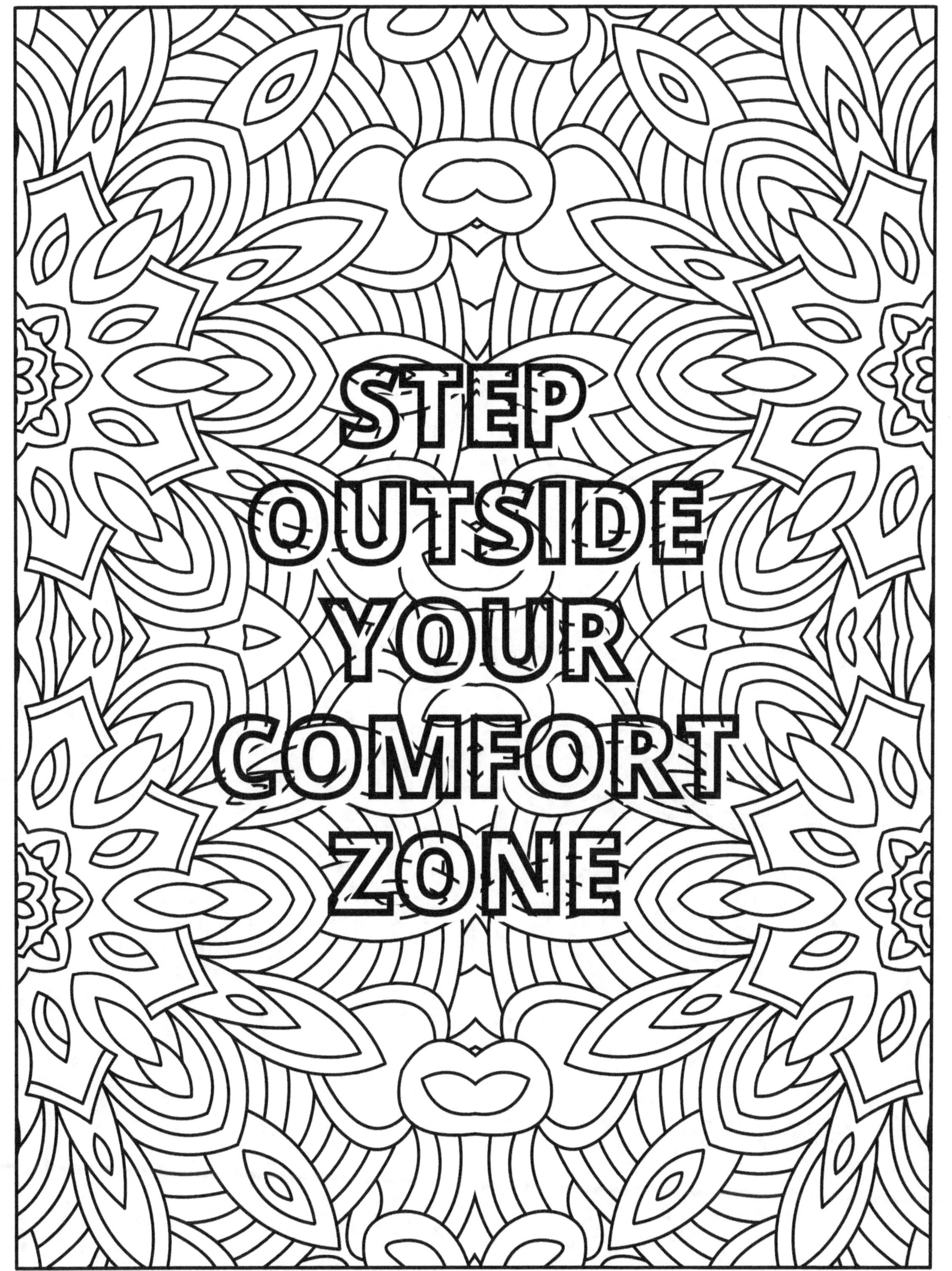

STEP
OUTSIDE
YOUR
COMFORT
ZONE

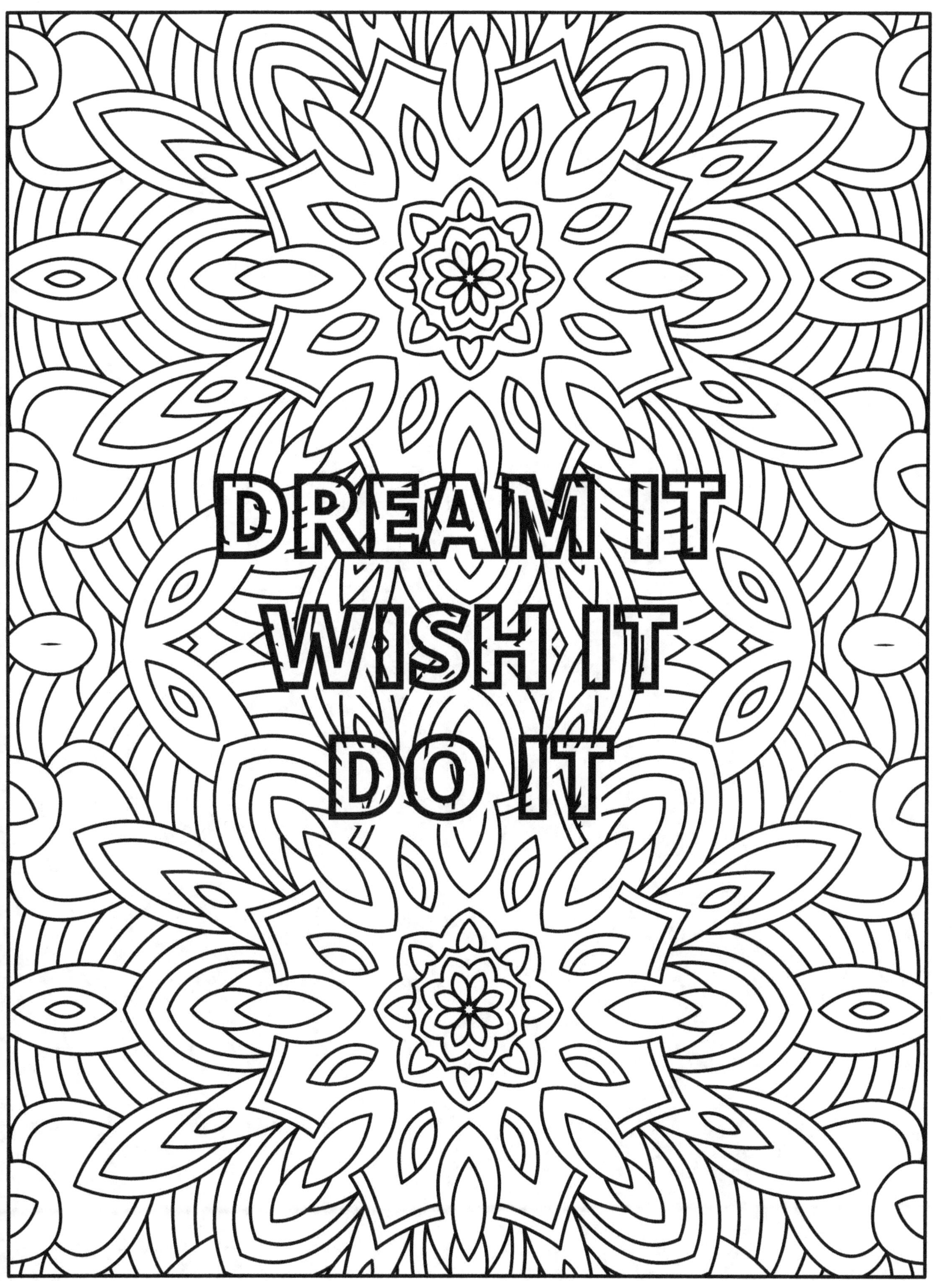

DREAM IT
WISH IT
DO IT

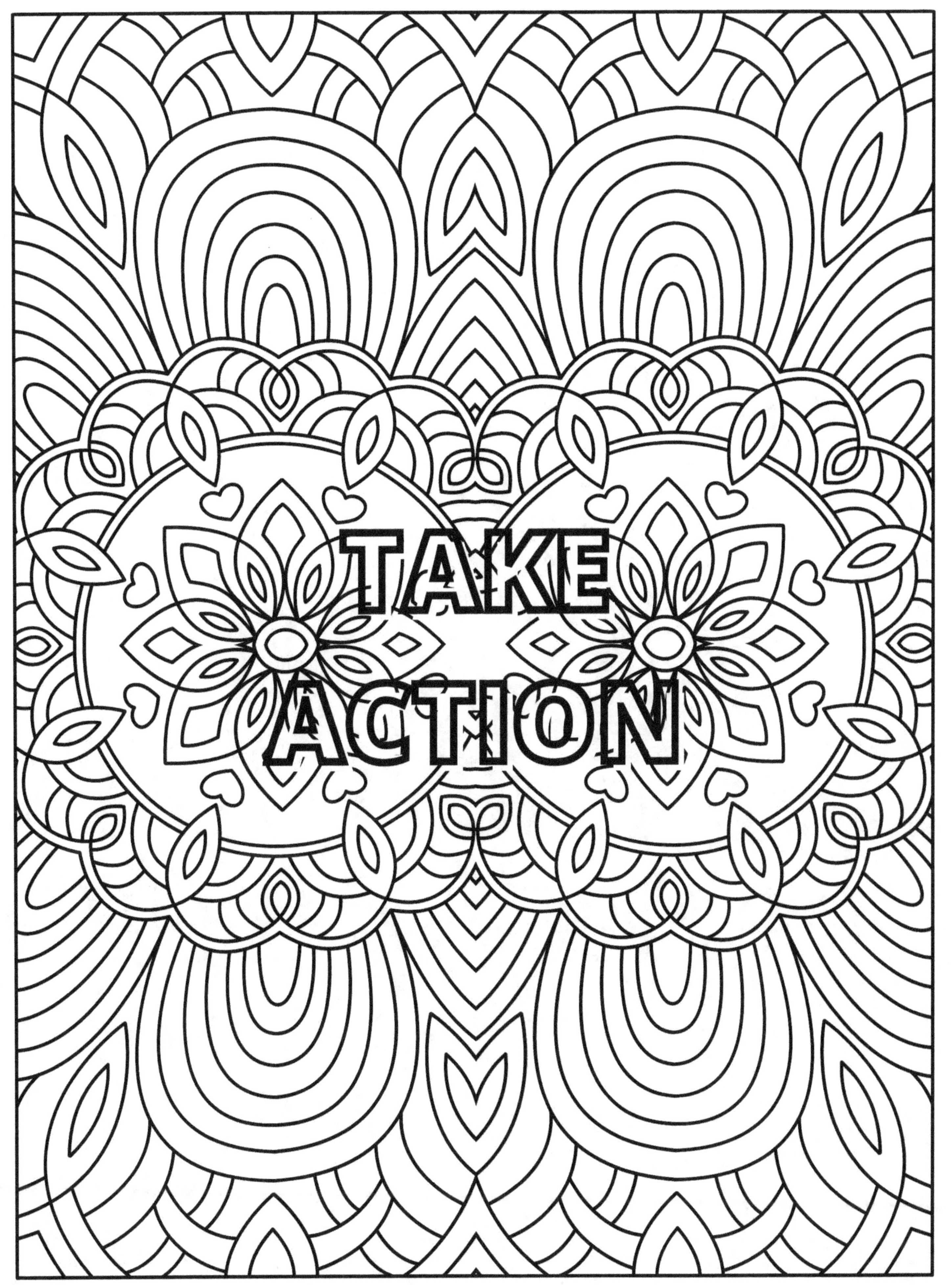

TAKE
ACTION

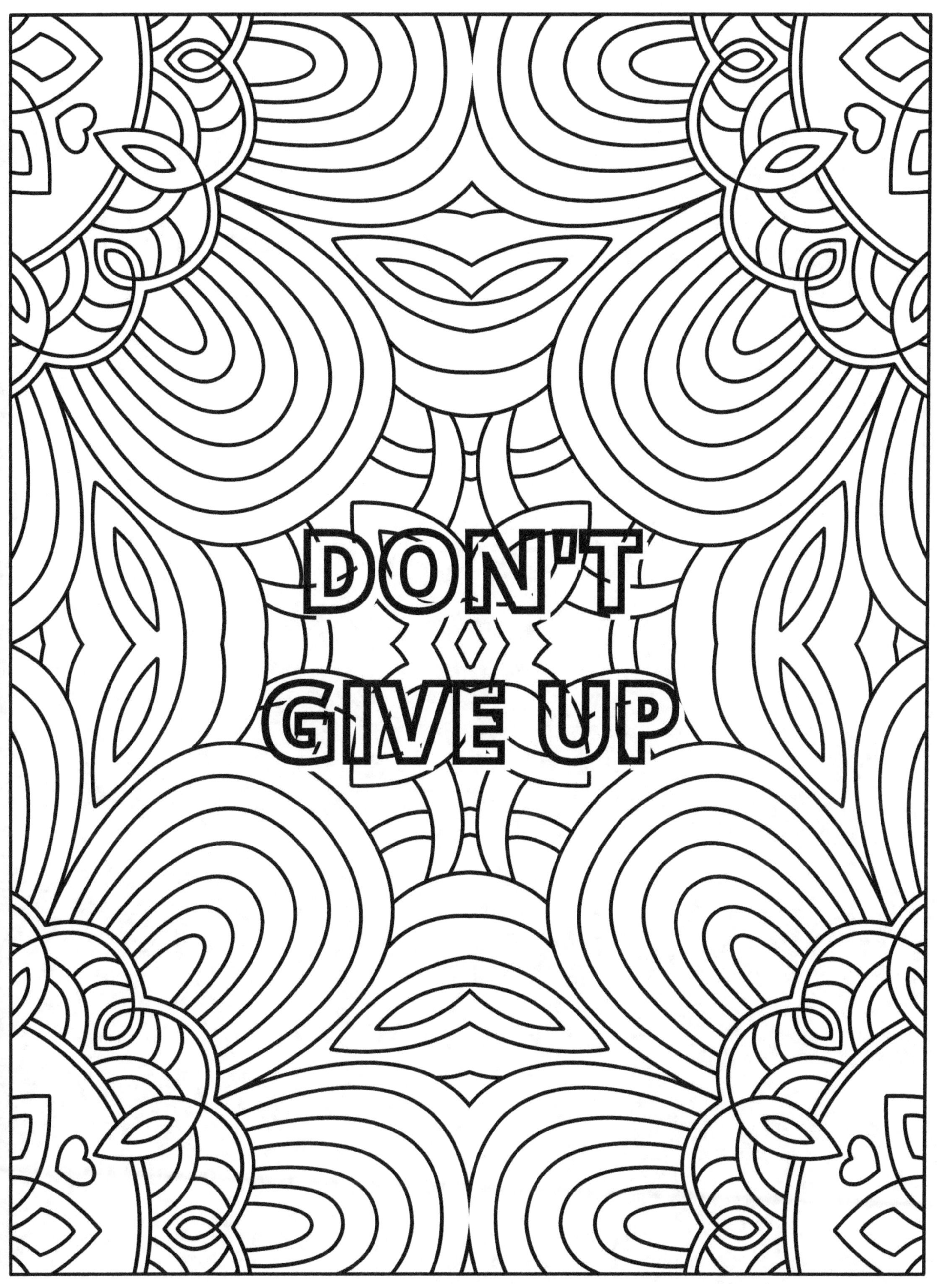
DON'T
GIVE UP

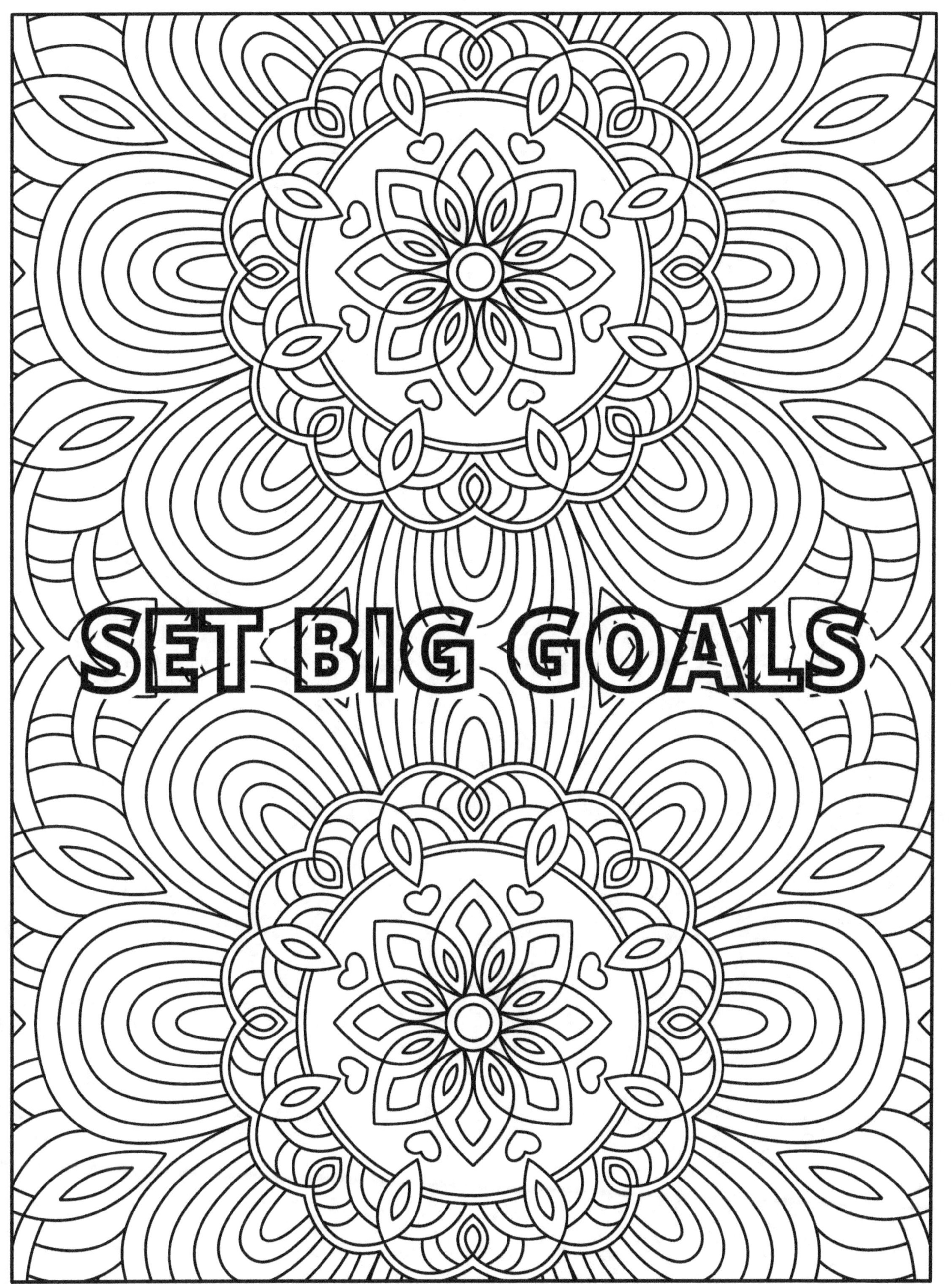
SET BIG GOALS

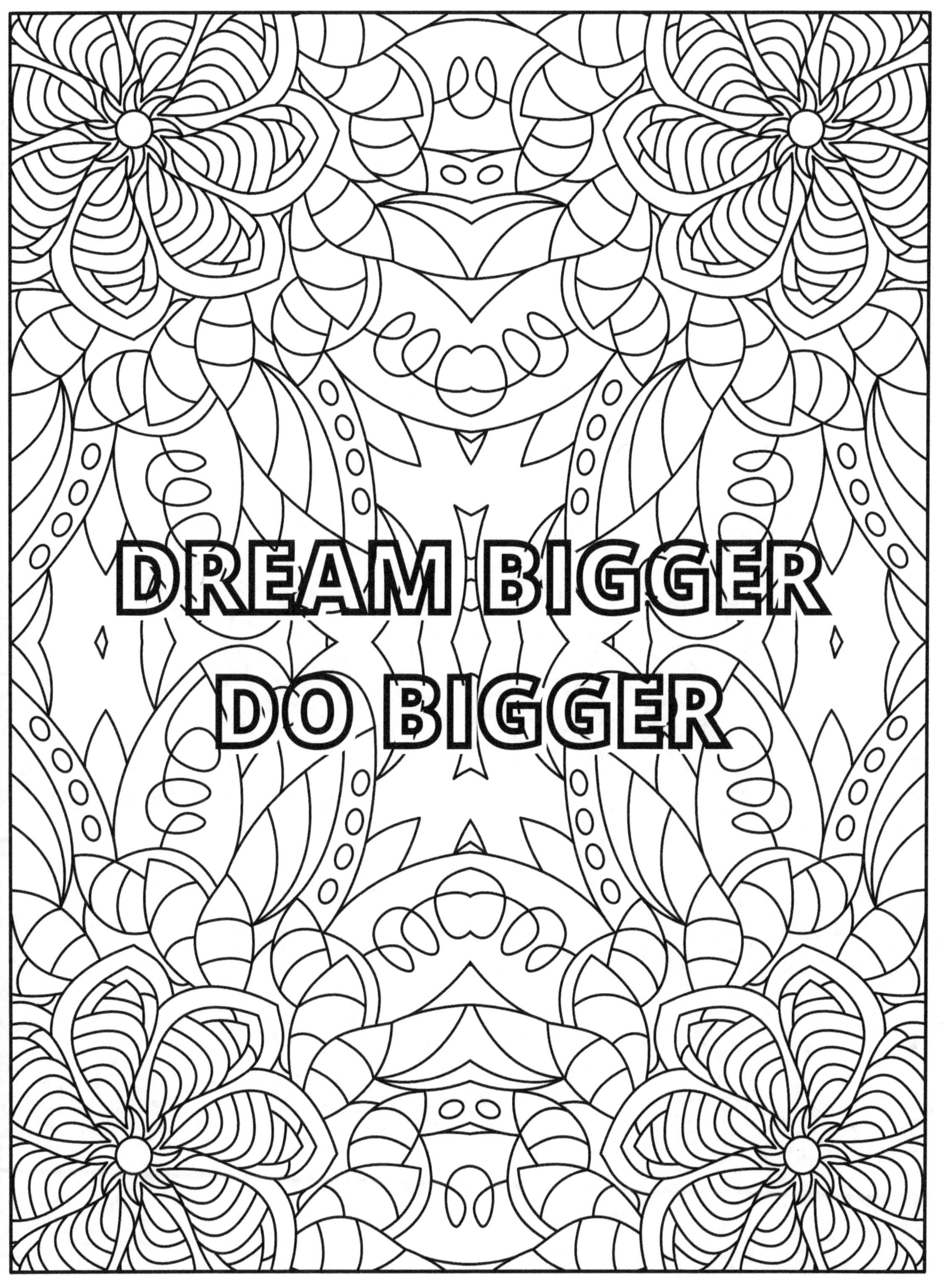

DREAM BIGGER
DO BIGGER

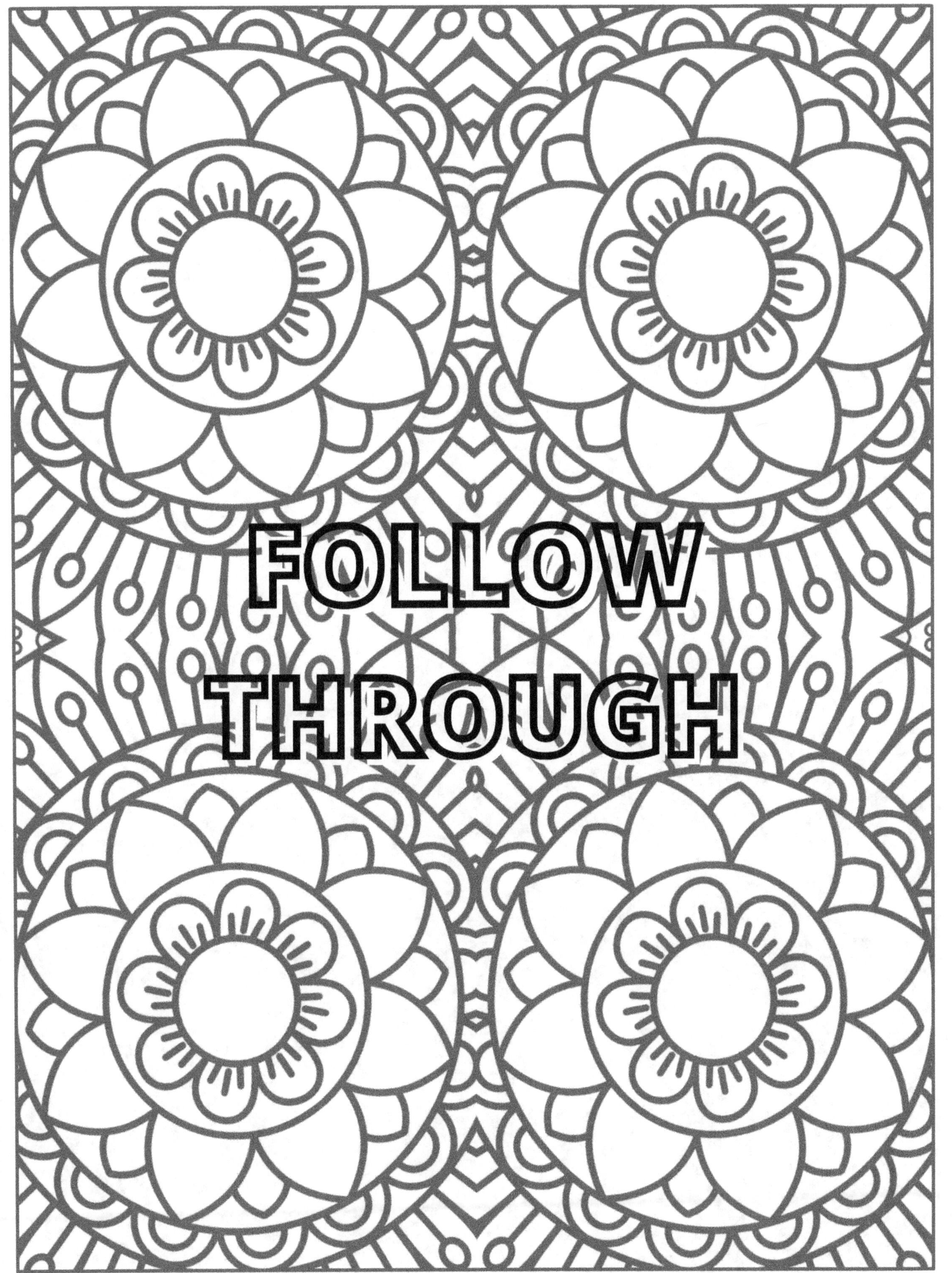
FOLLOW
THROUGH

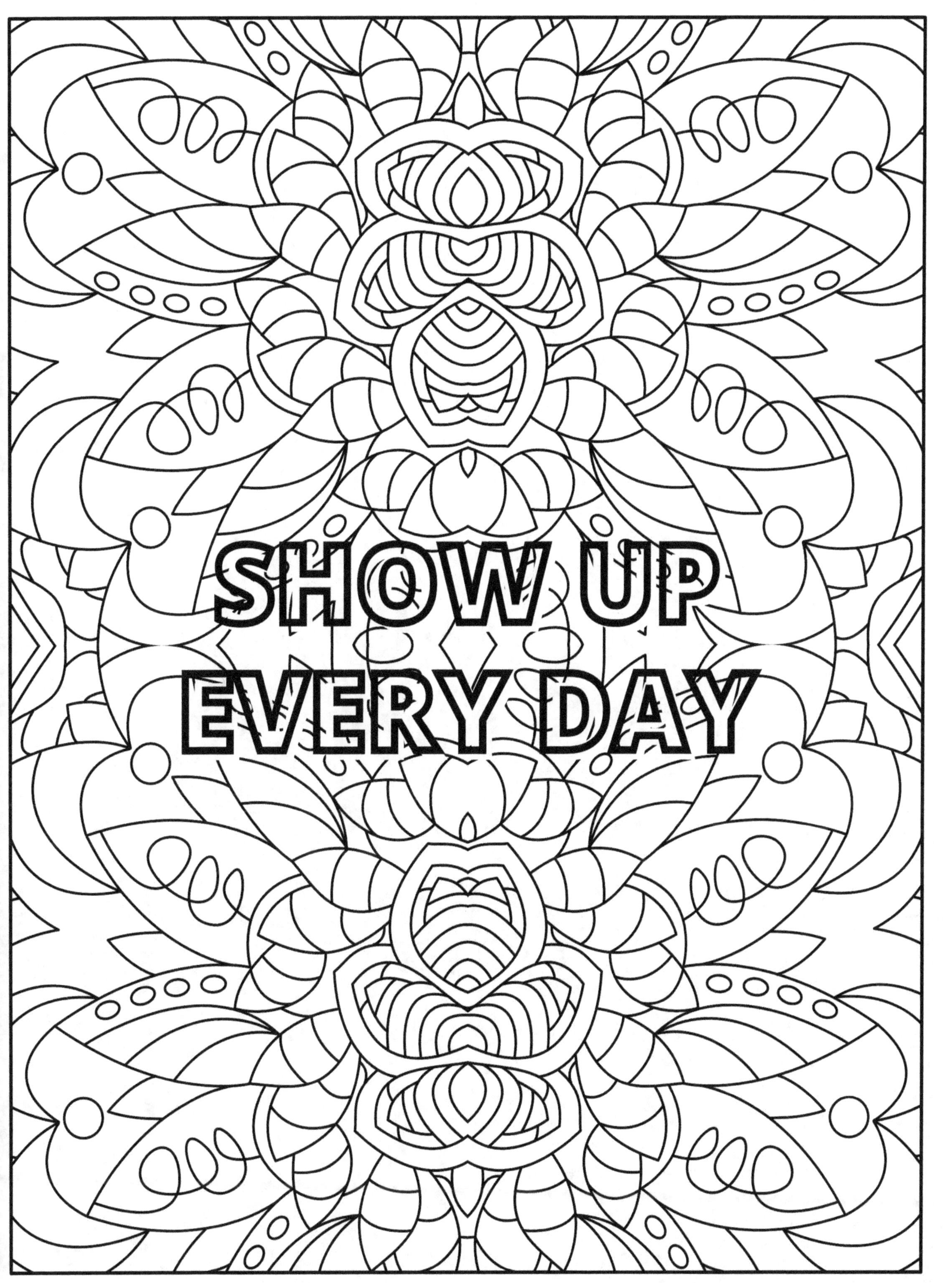

SHOW UP
EVERY DAY

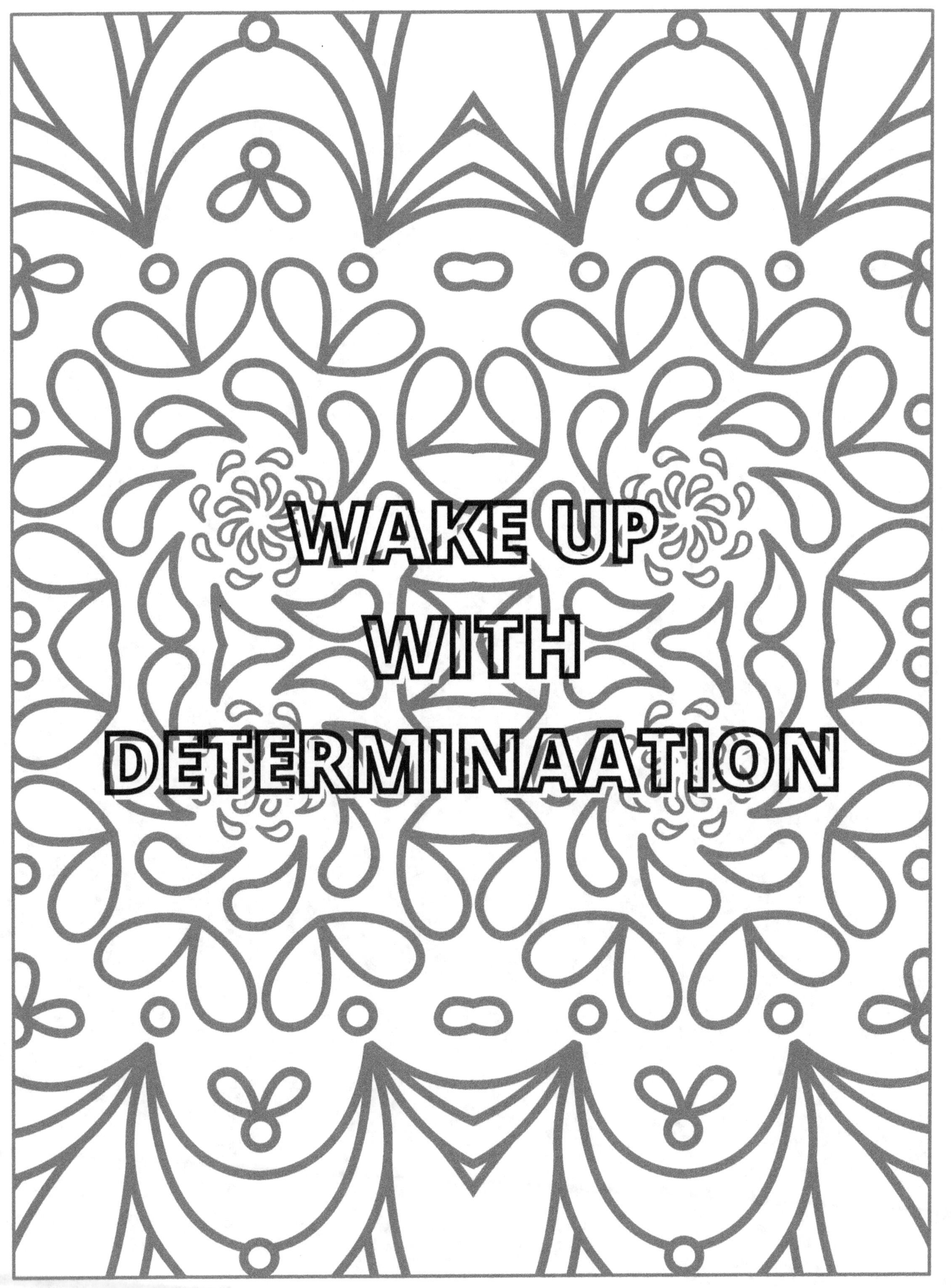

WAKE UP
WITH
DETERMINAATION

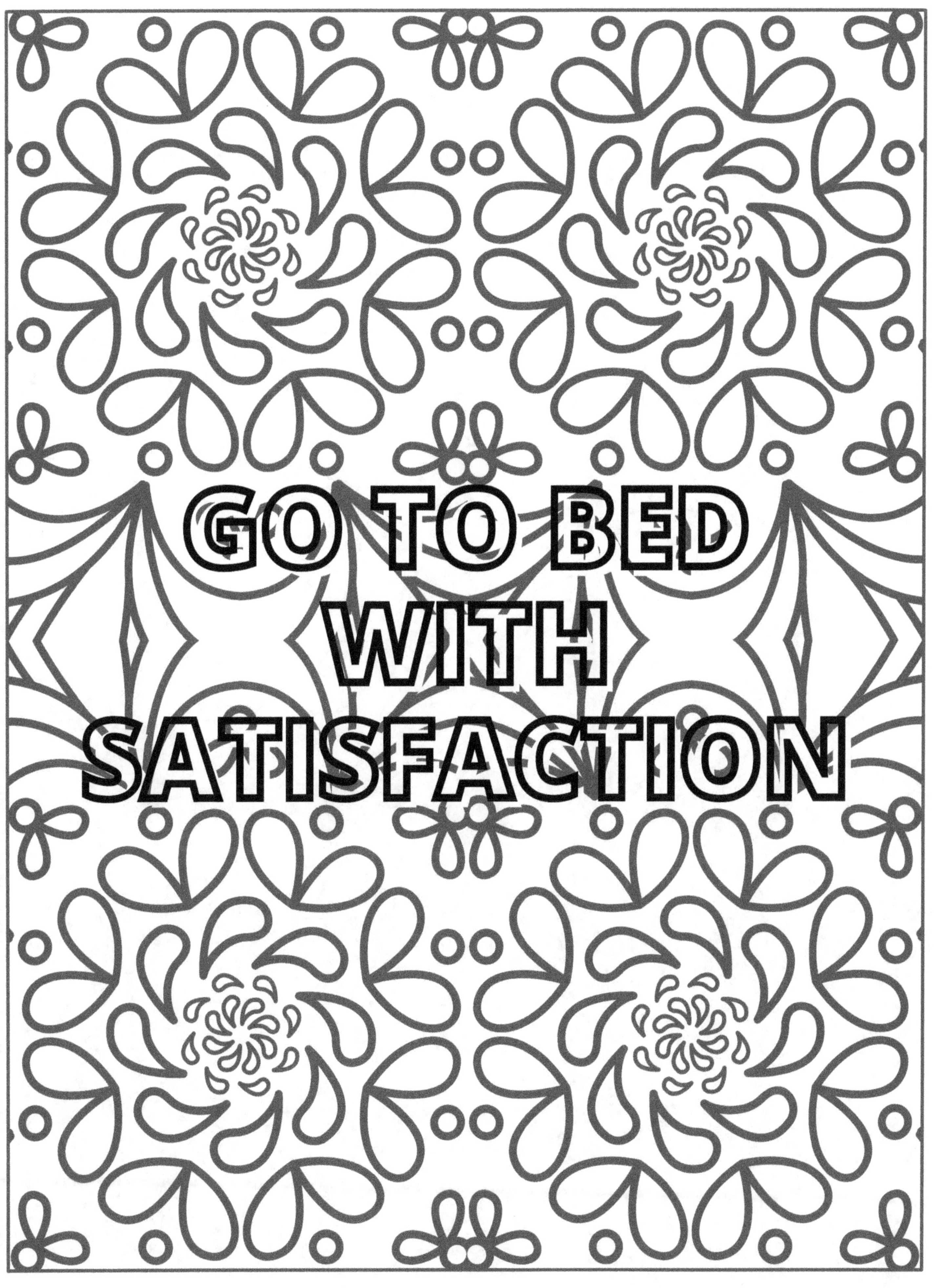
GO TO BED
WITH
SATISFACTION

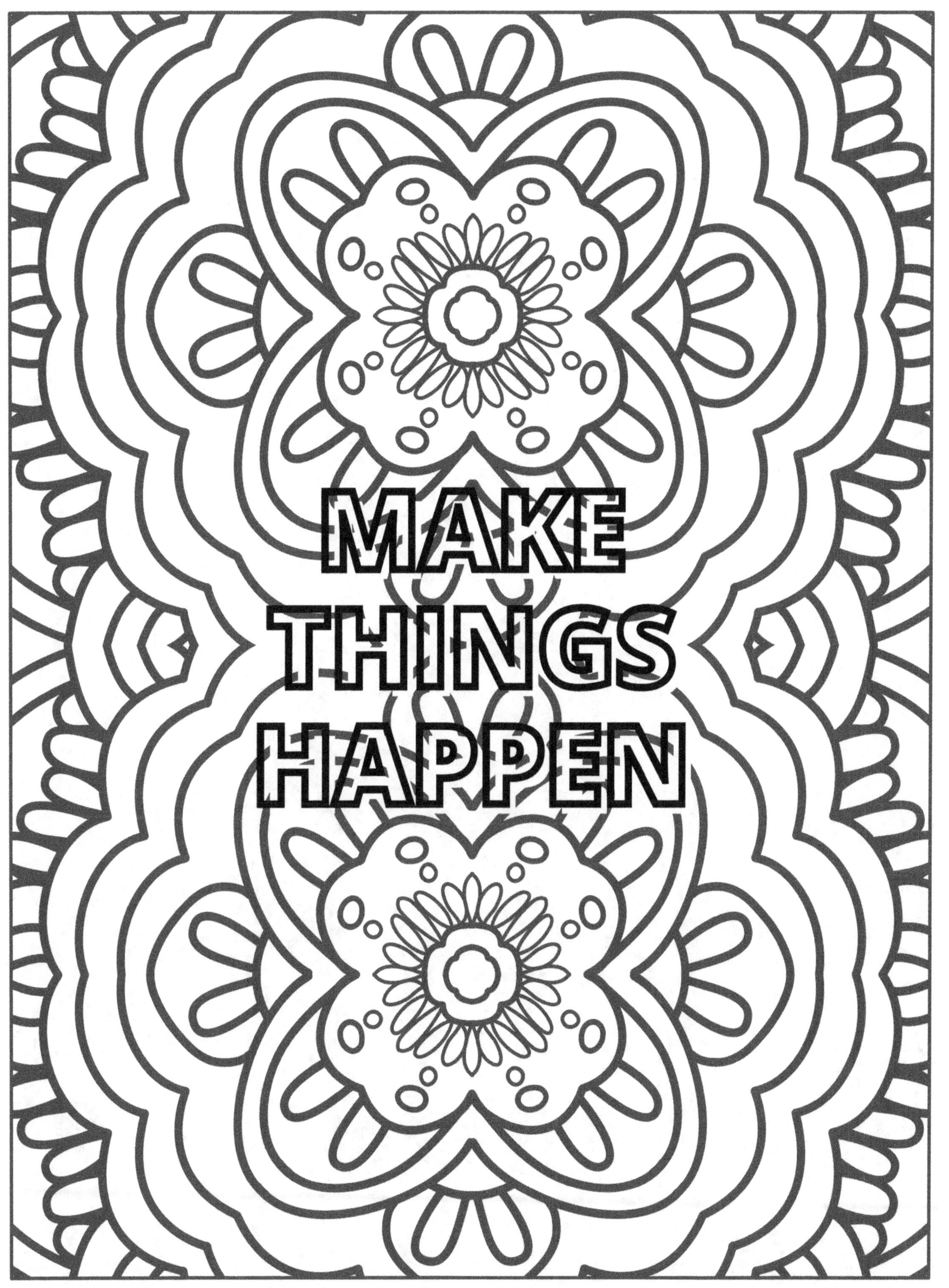

MAKE
THINGS
HAPPEN

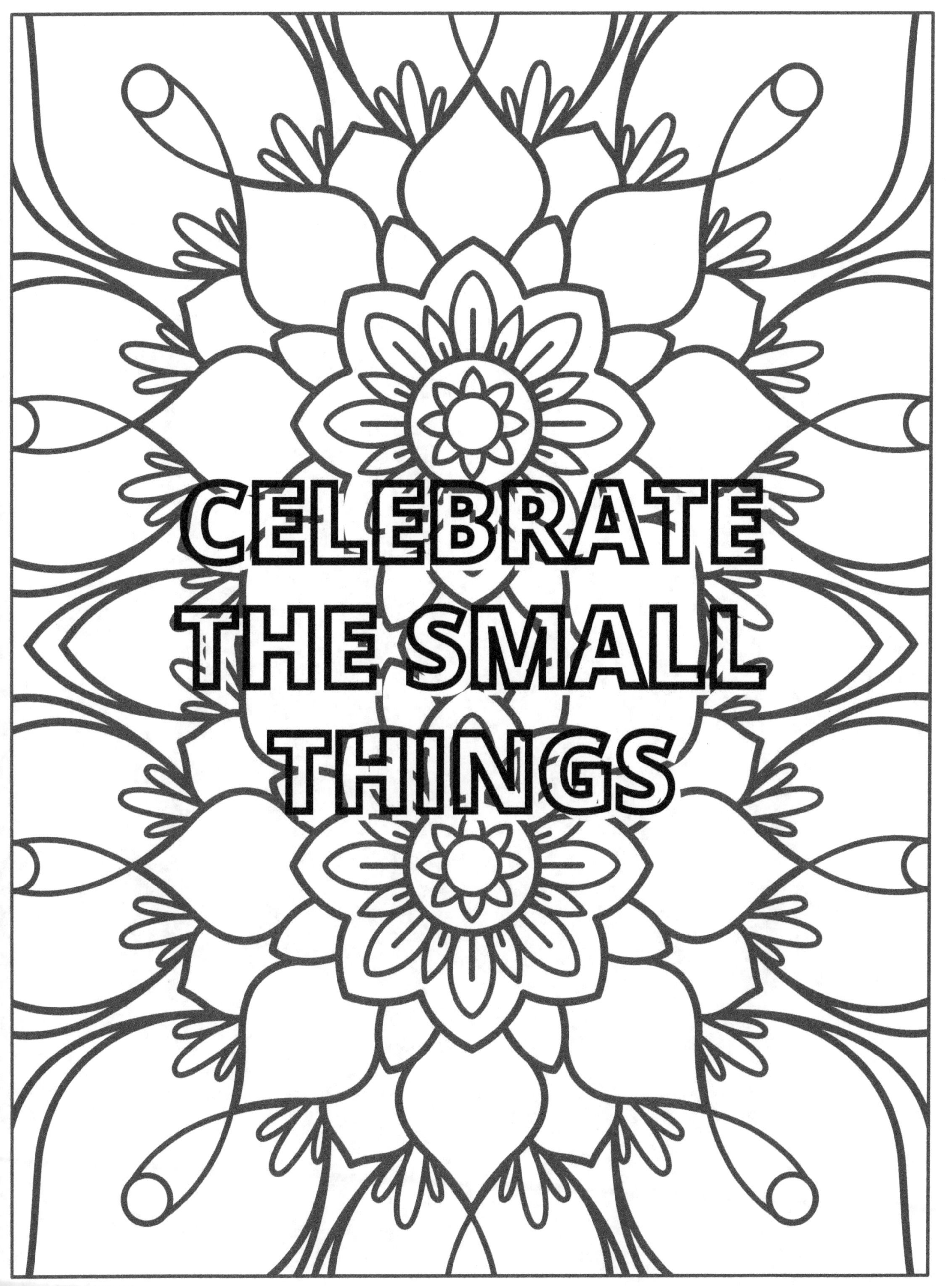

CELEBRATE
THE SMALL
THINGS

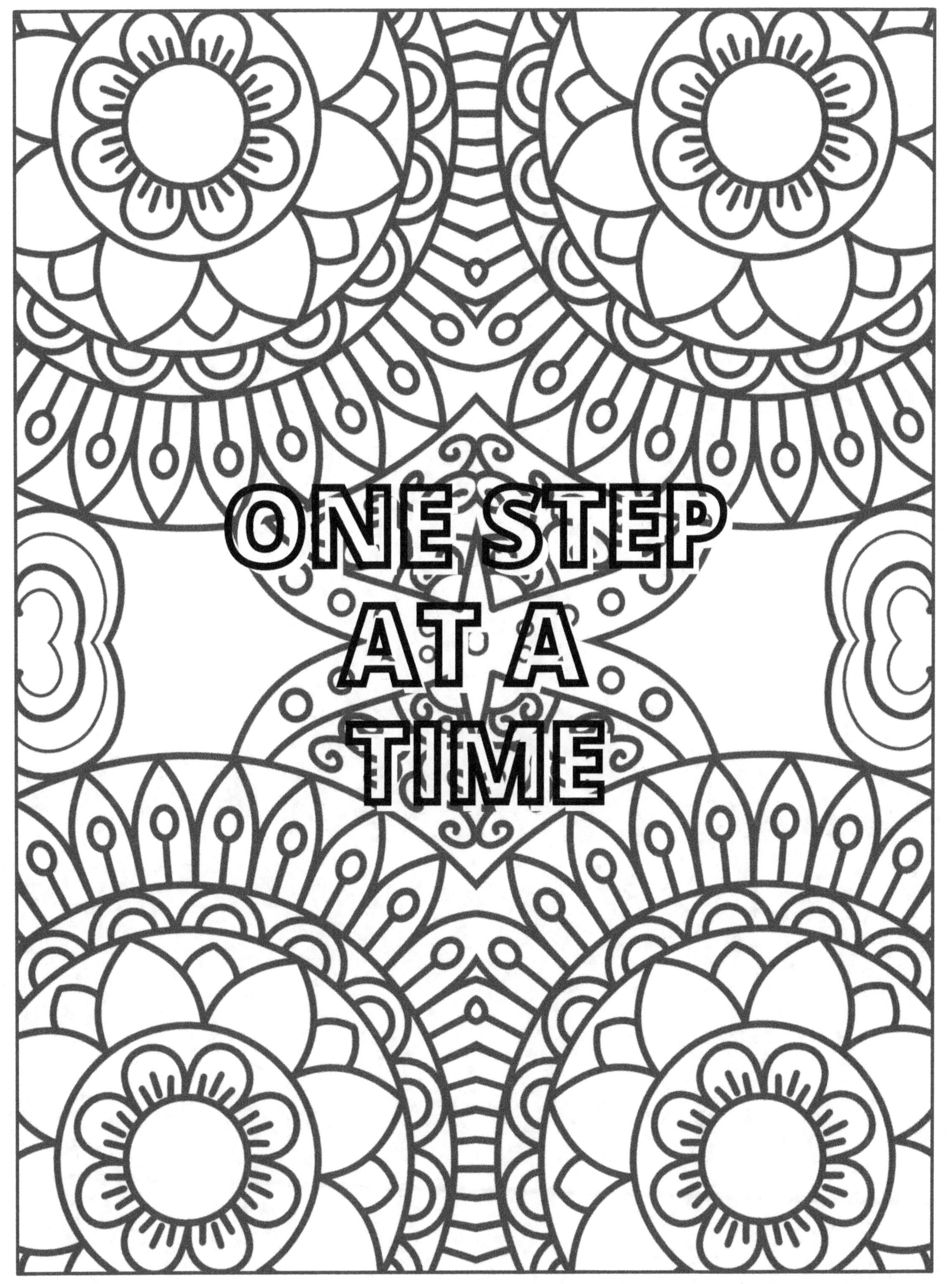

ONE STEP
AT A
TIME

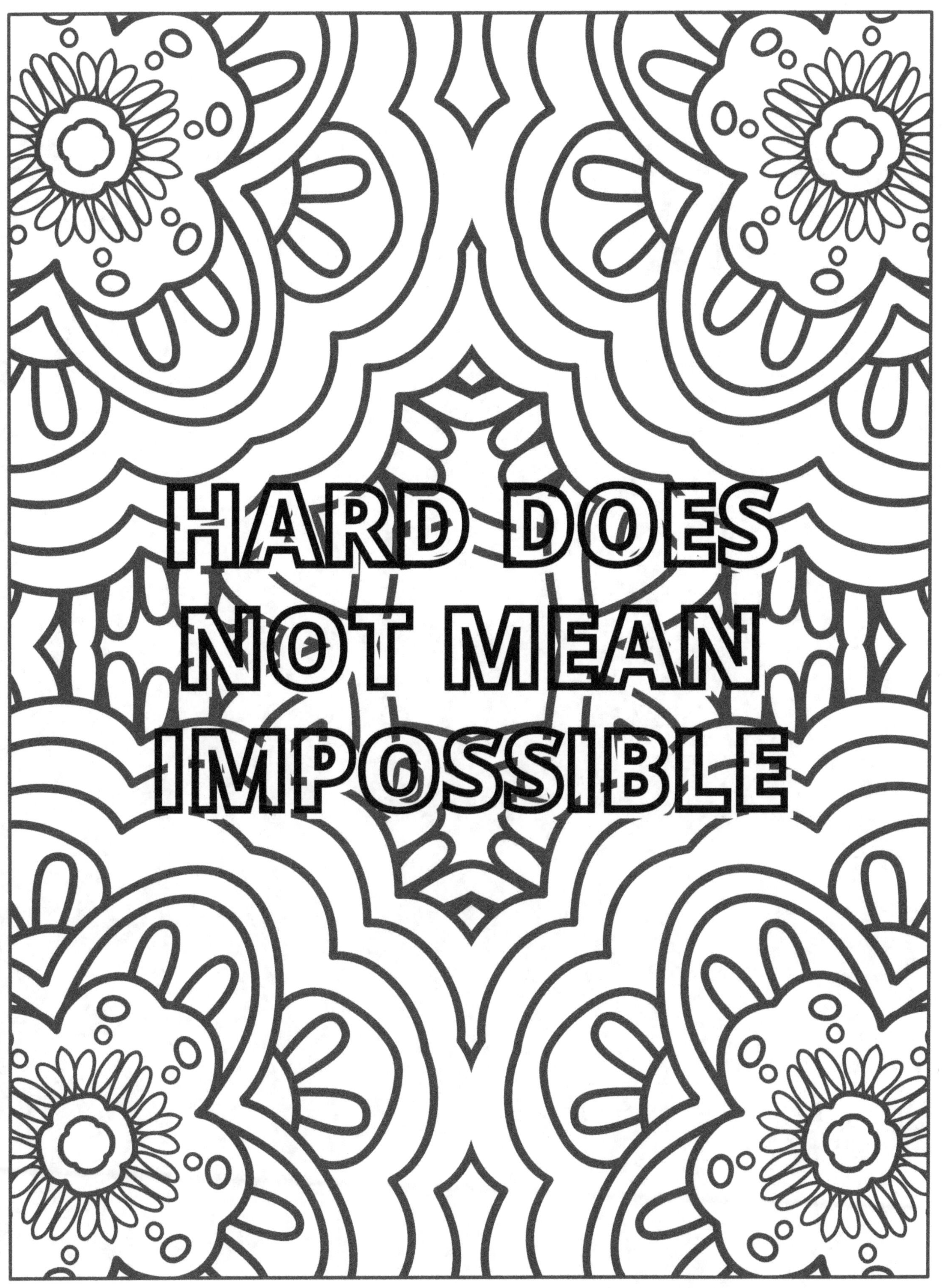
HARD DOES
NOT MEAN
IMPOSSIBLE

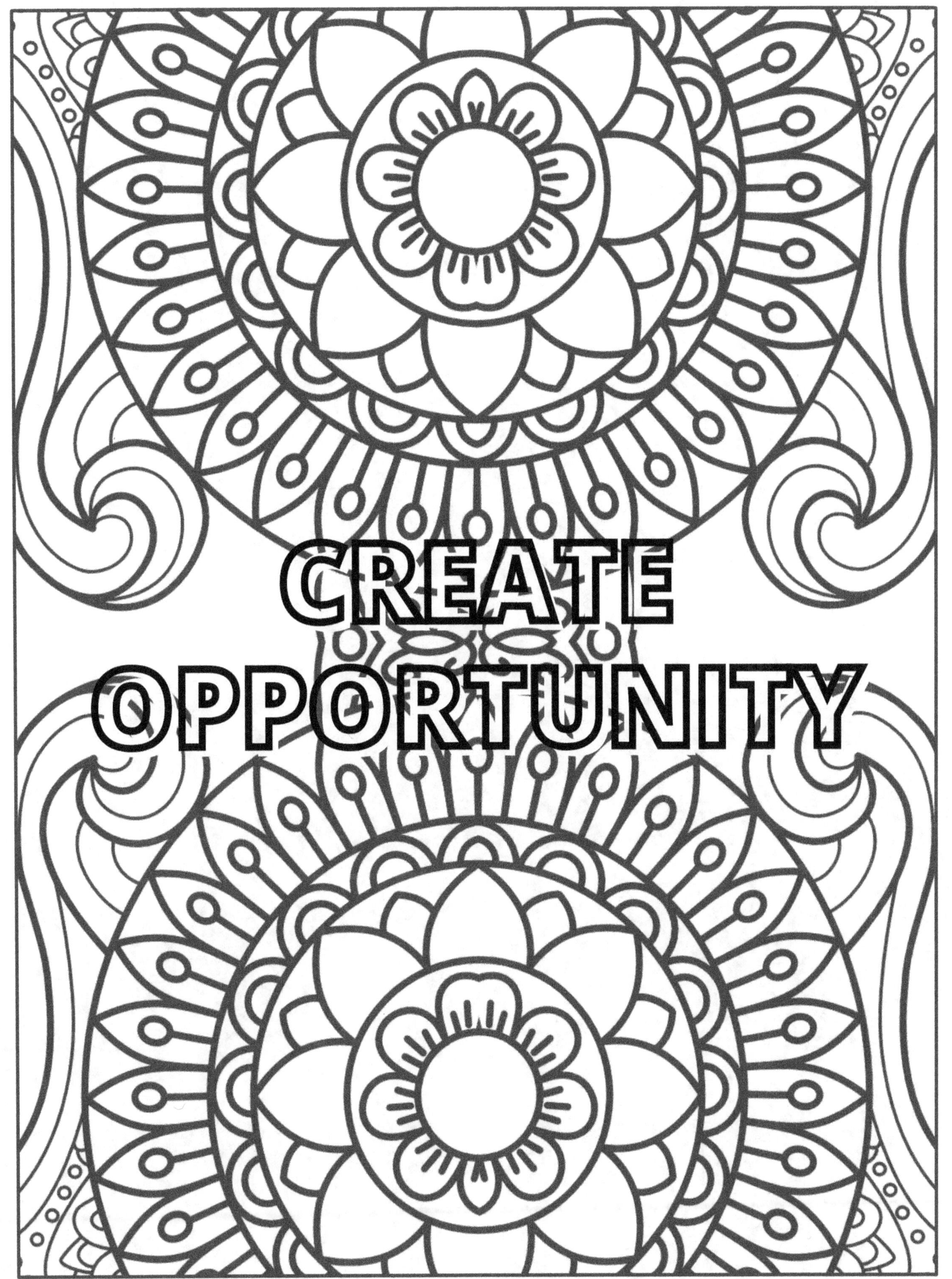

CREATE
OPPORTUNITY

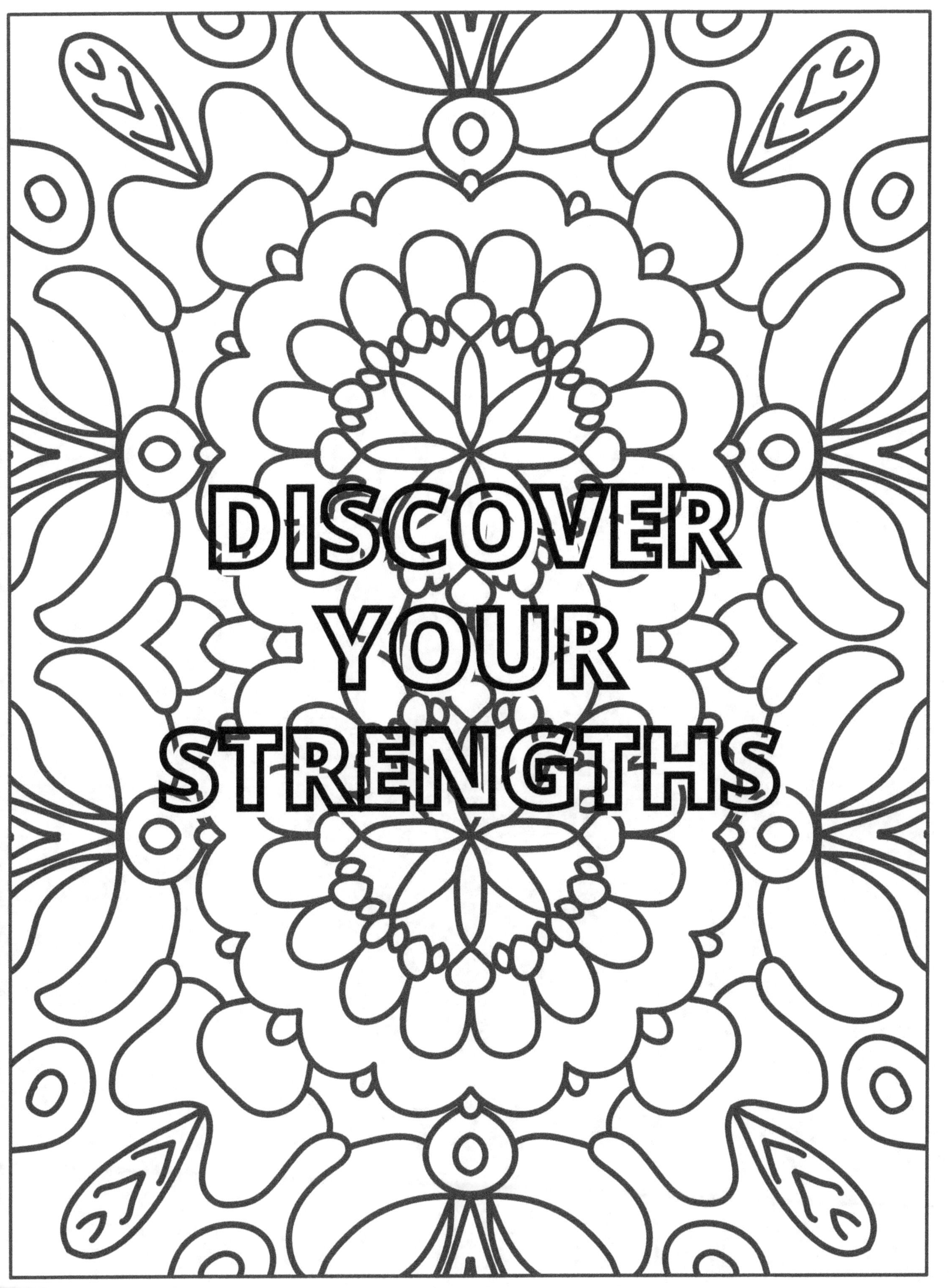

DISCOVER
YOUR
STRENGTHS

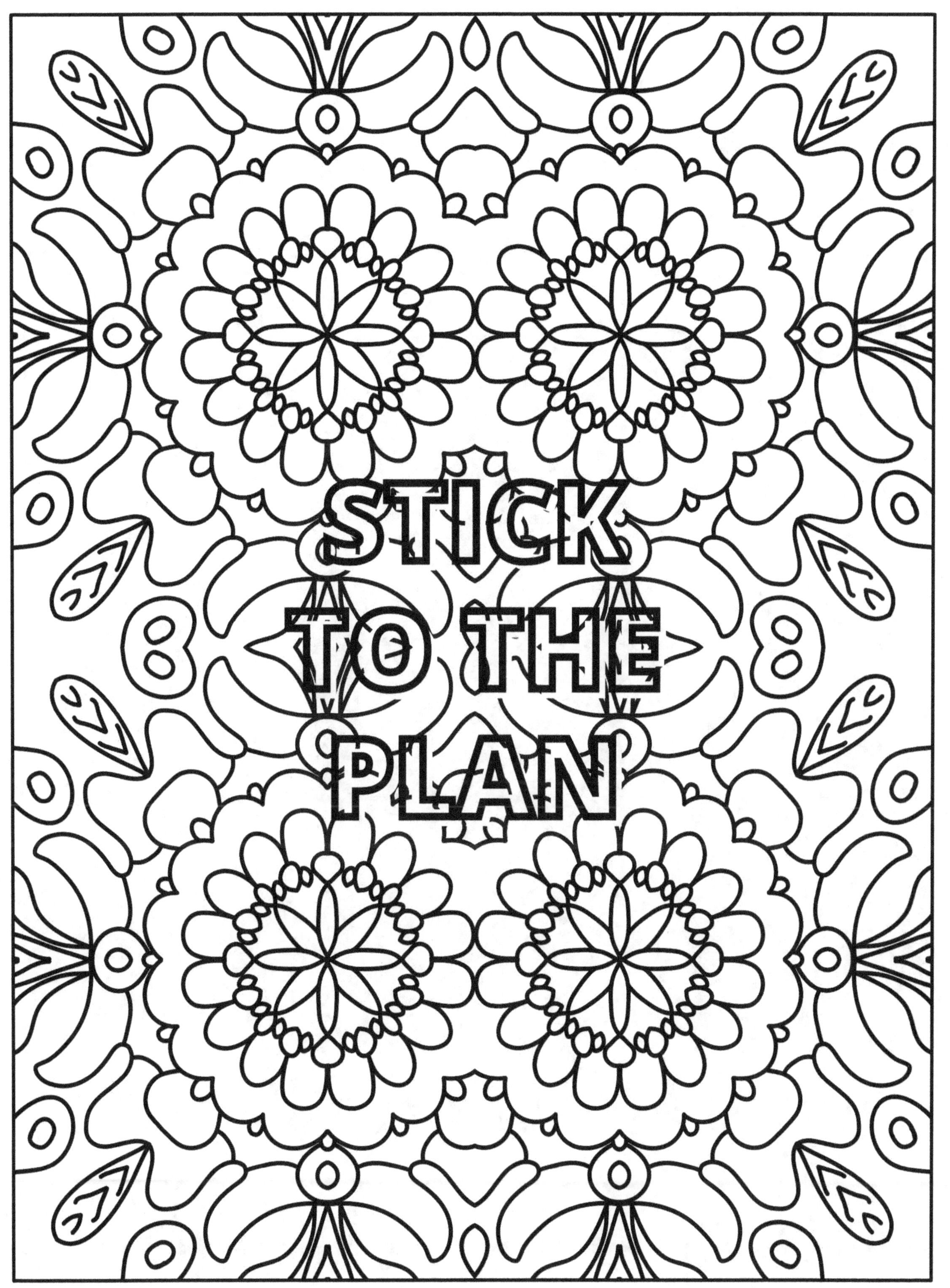

STICK
TO THE
PLAN

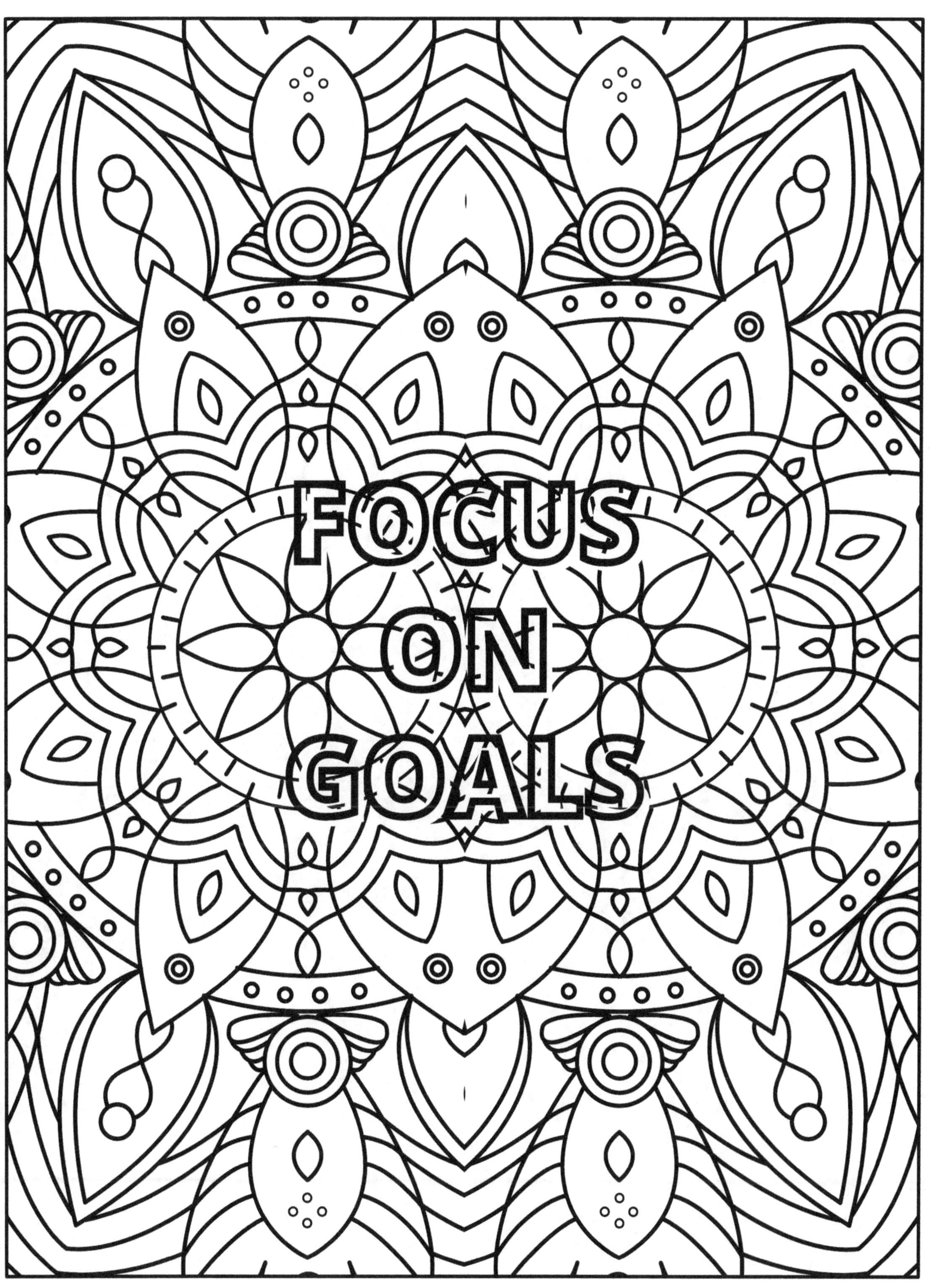

FOCUS
ON
GOALS

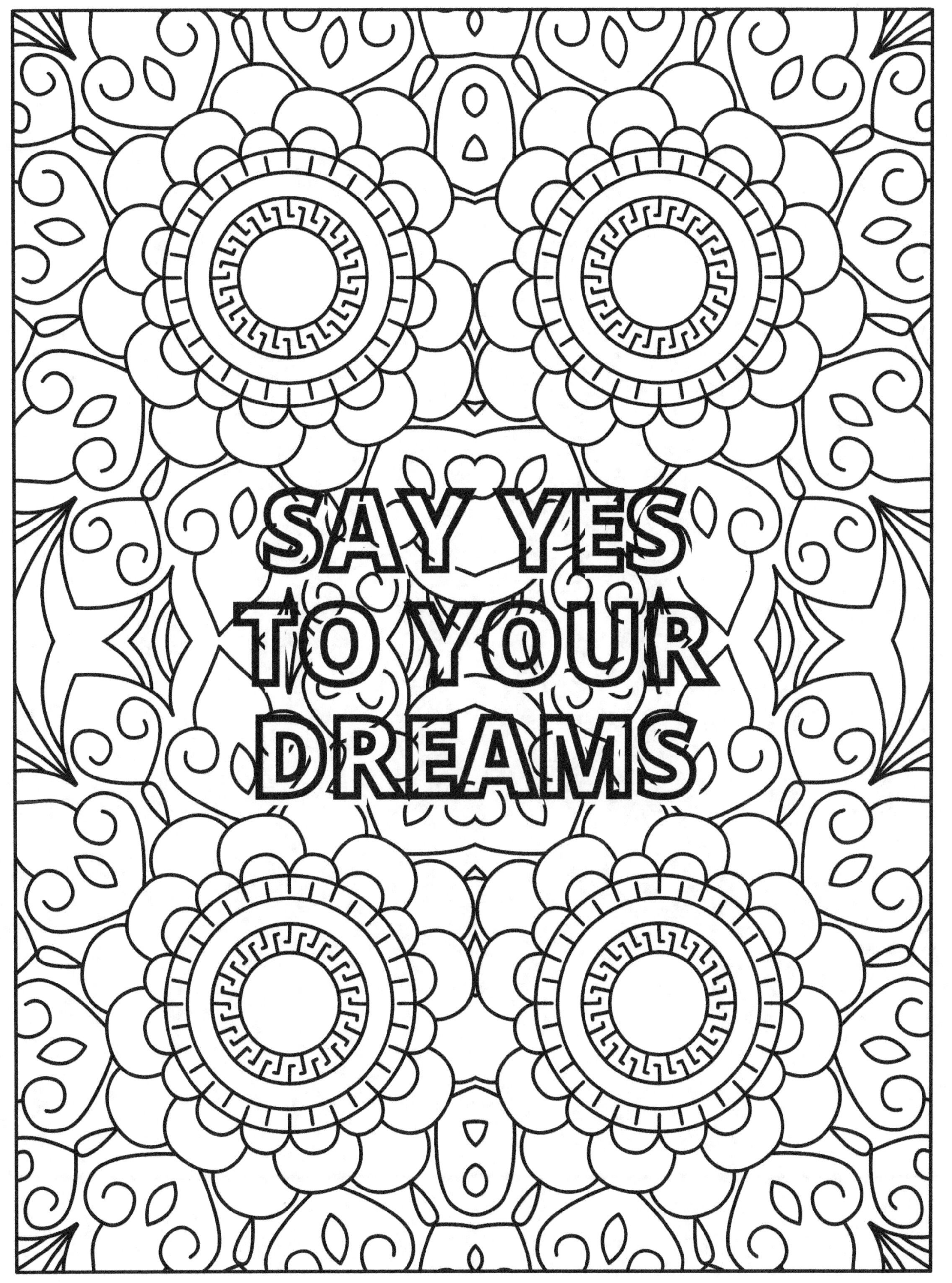SAY YES
TO YOUR
DREAMS

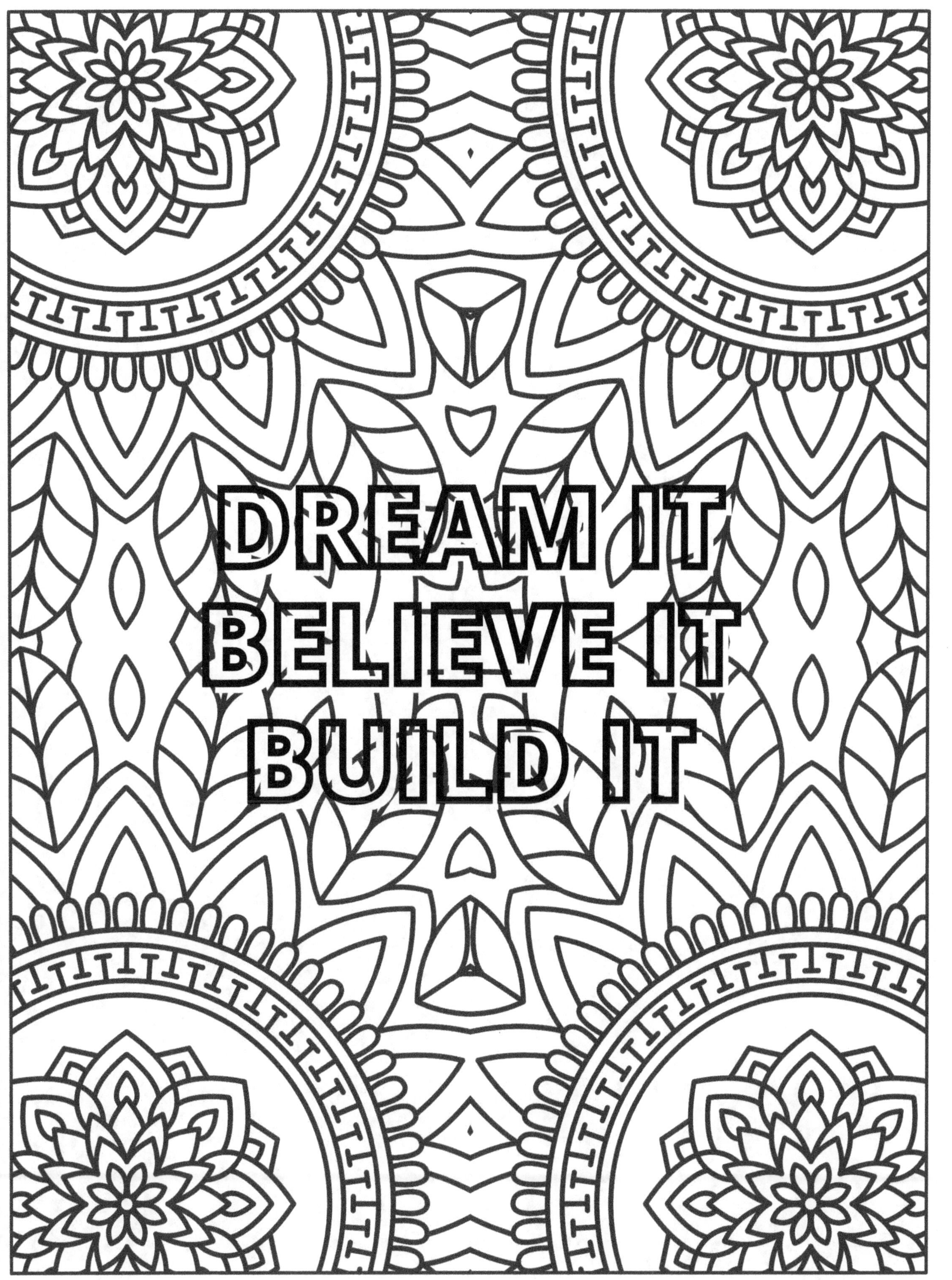

DREAM IT
BELIEVE IT
BUILD IT

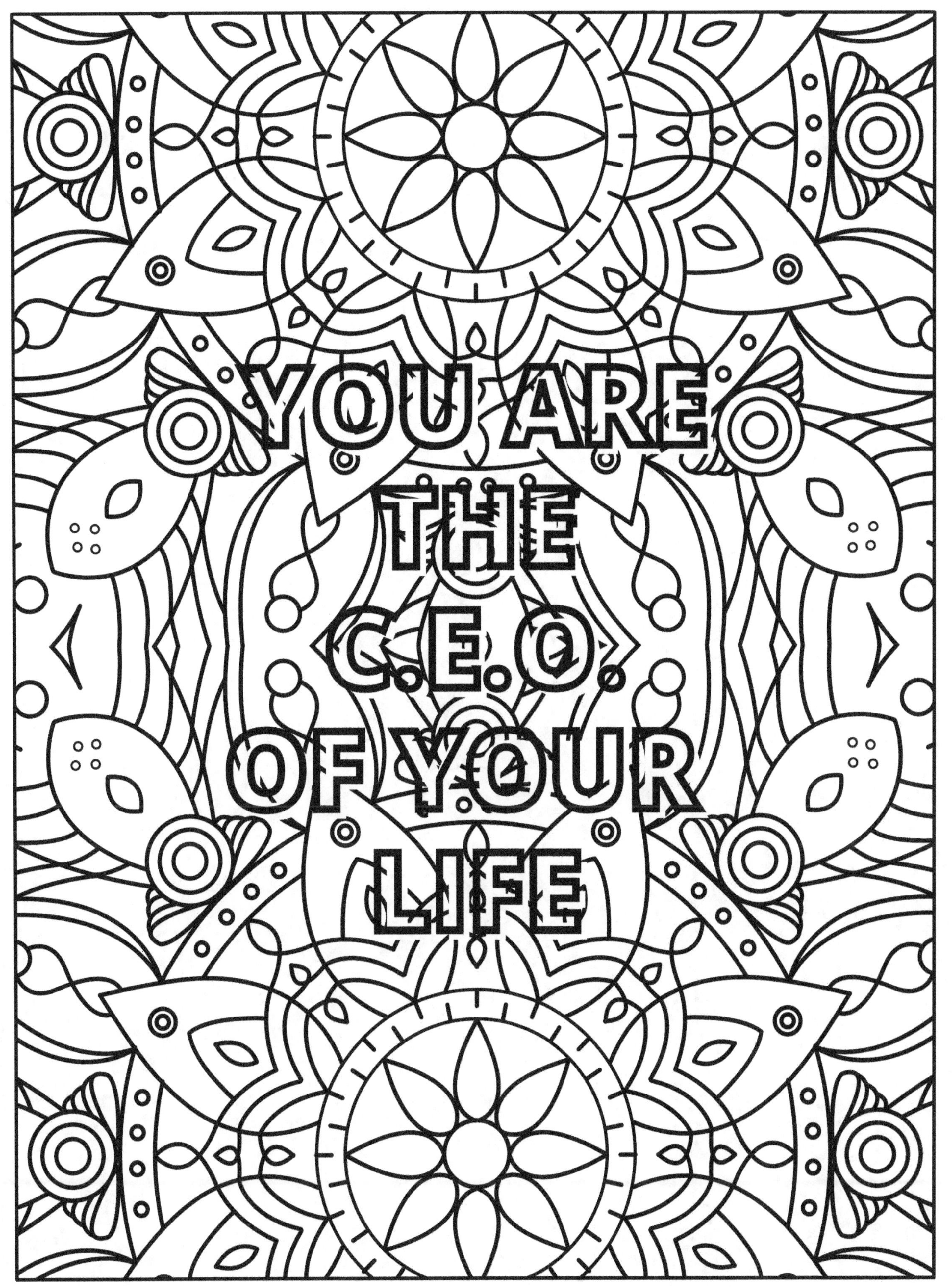

YOU ARE
THE
C.E.O.
OF YOUR
LIFE

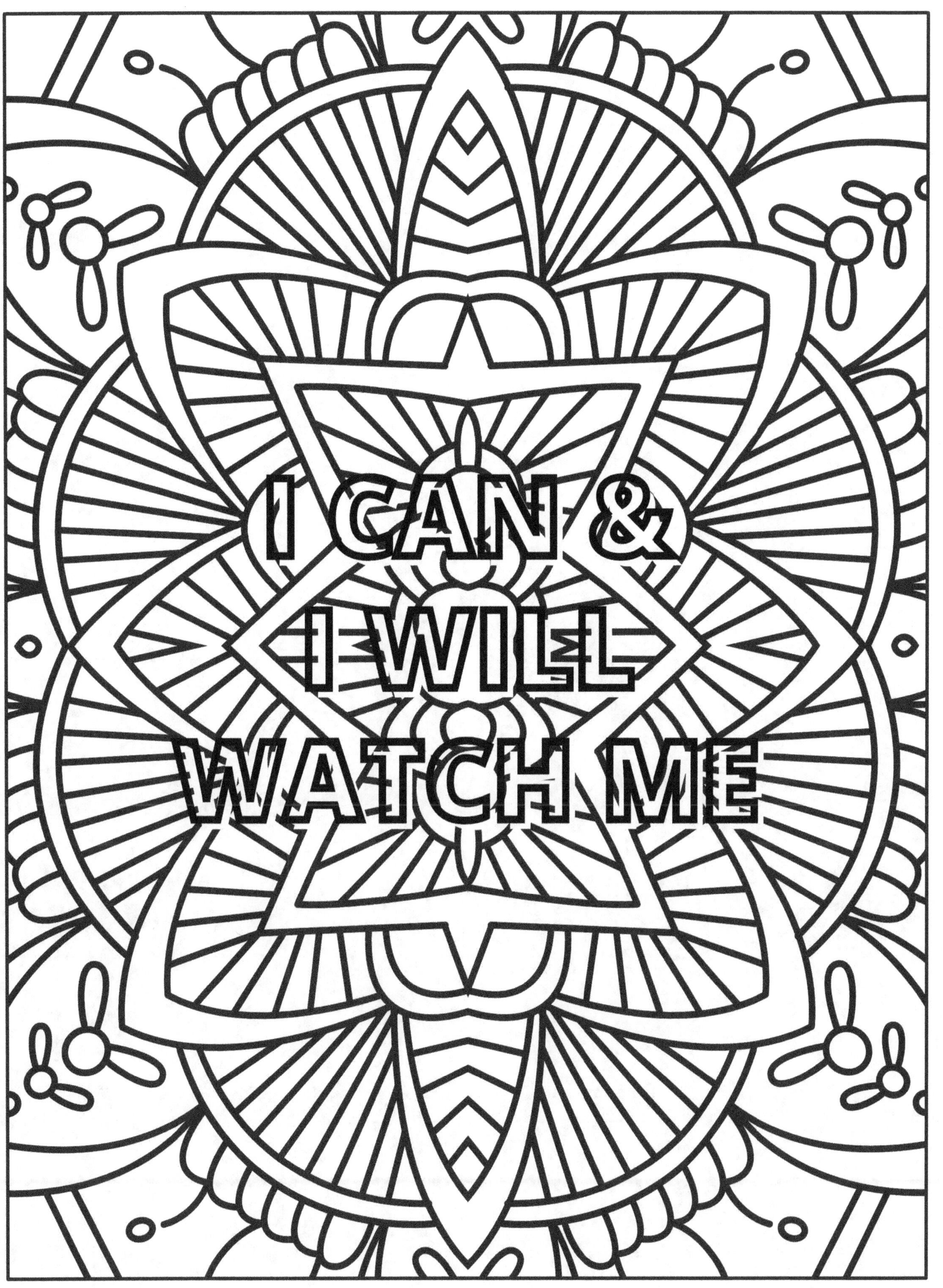

I CAN &
I WILL
WATCH ME

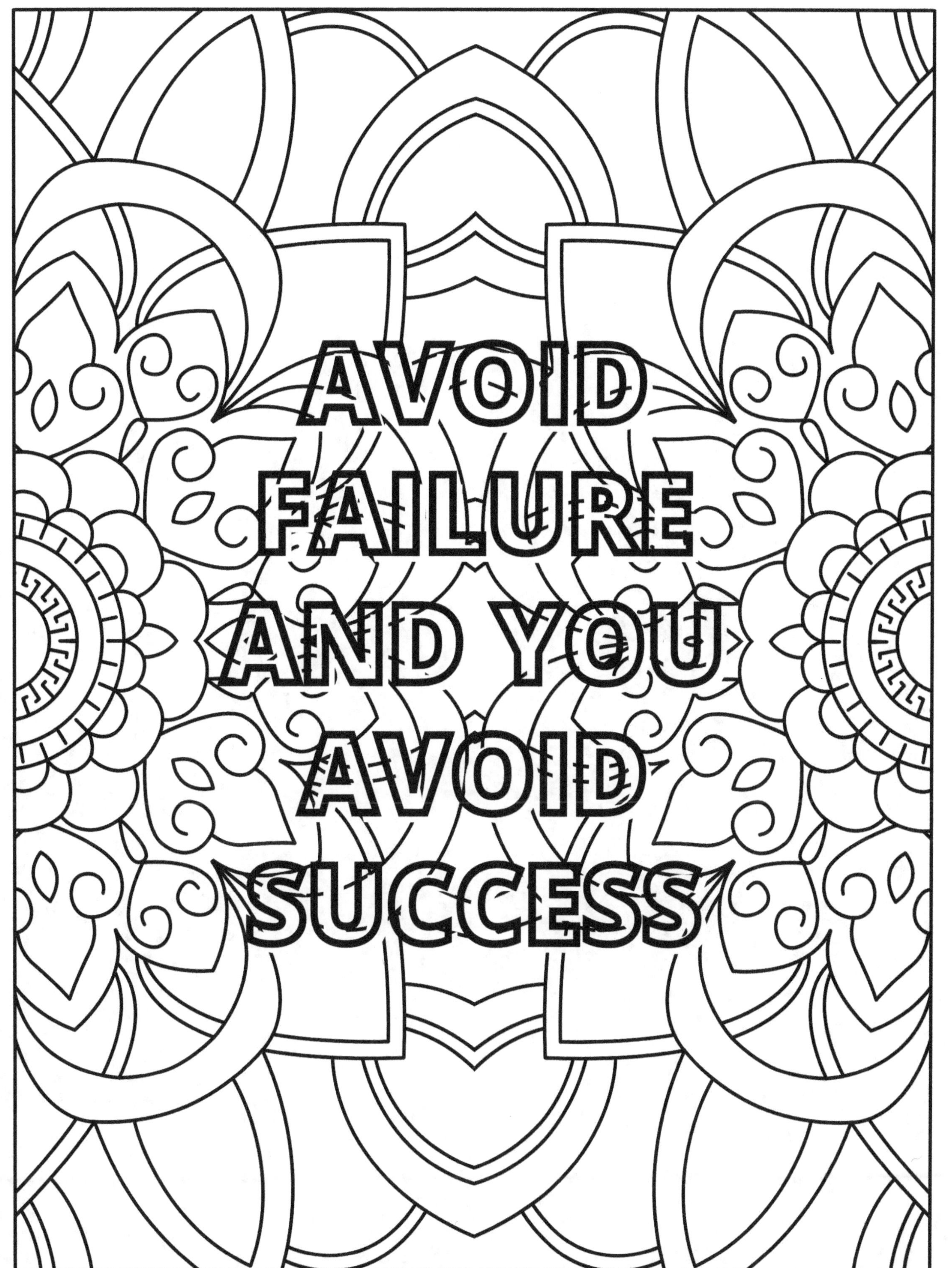

AVOID
FAILURE
AND YOU
AVOID
SUCCESS

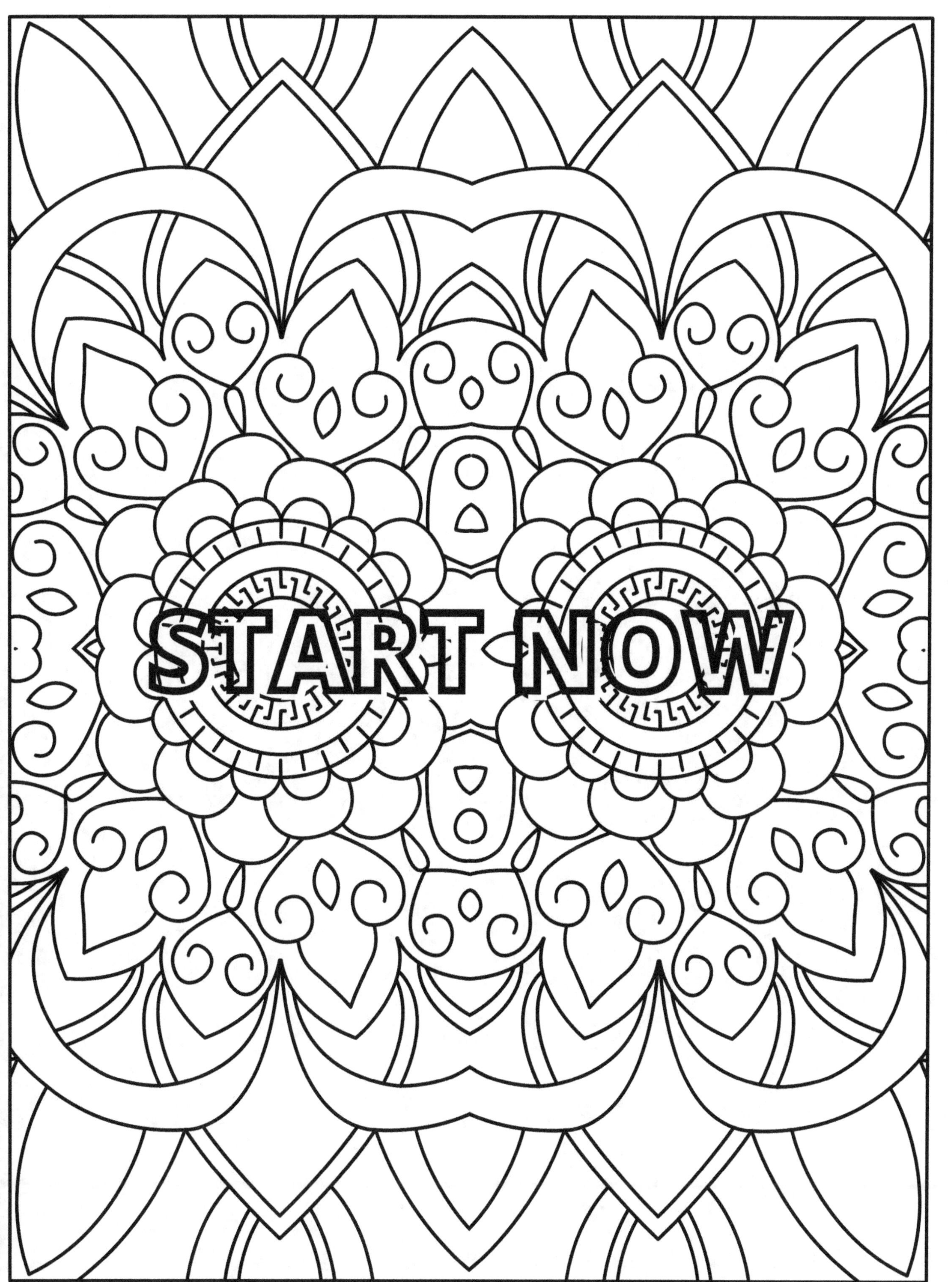
START NOW

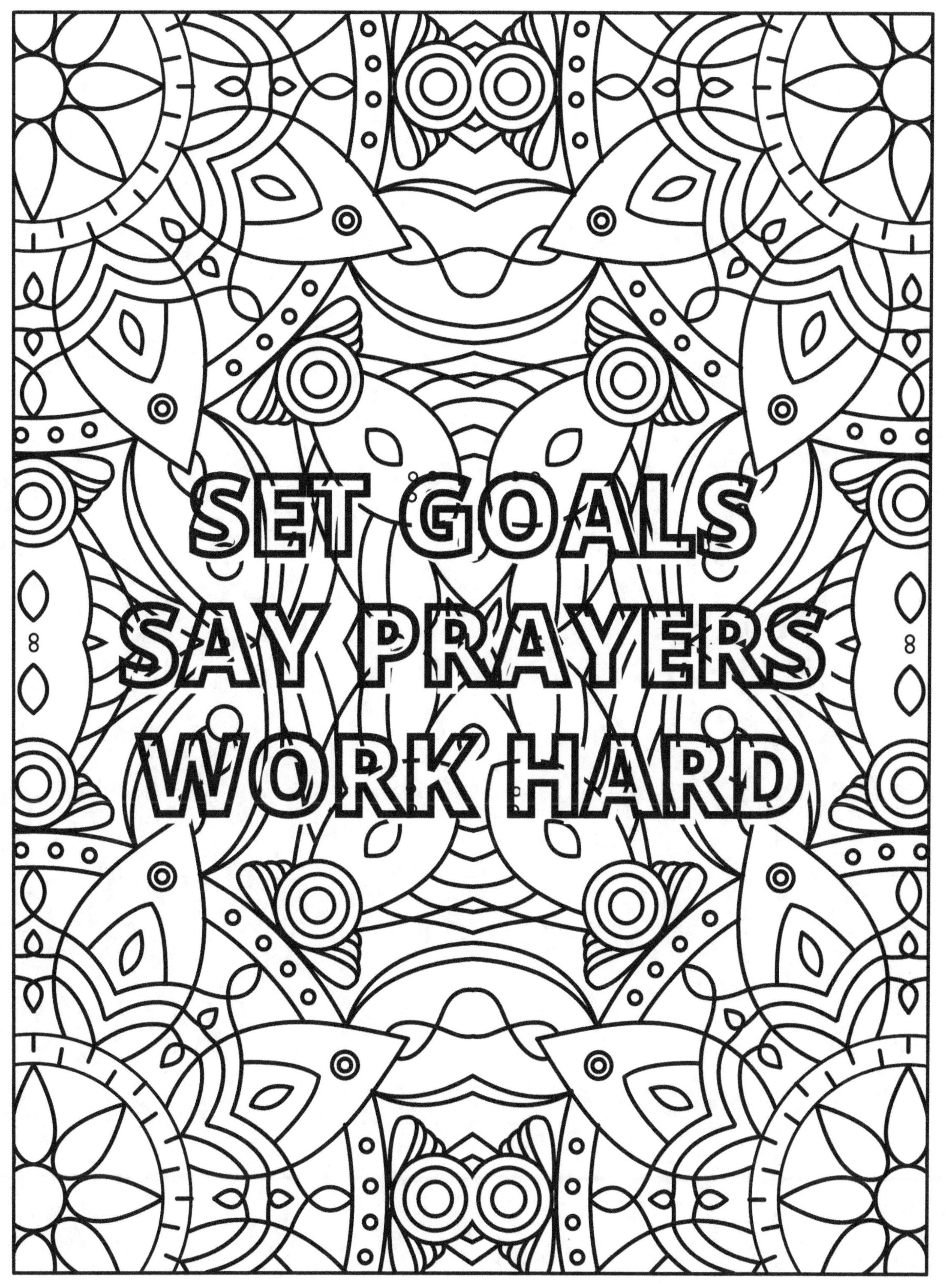

SET GOALS
SAY PRAYERS
WORK HARD

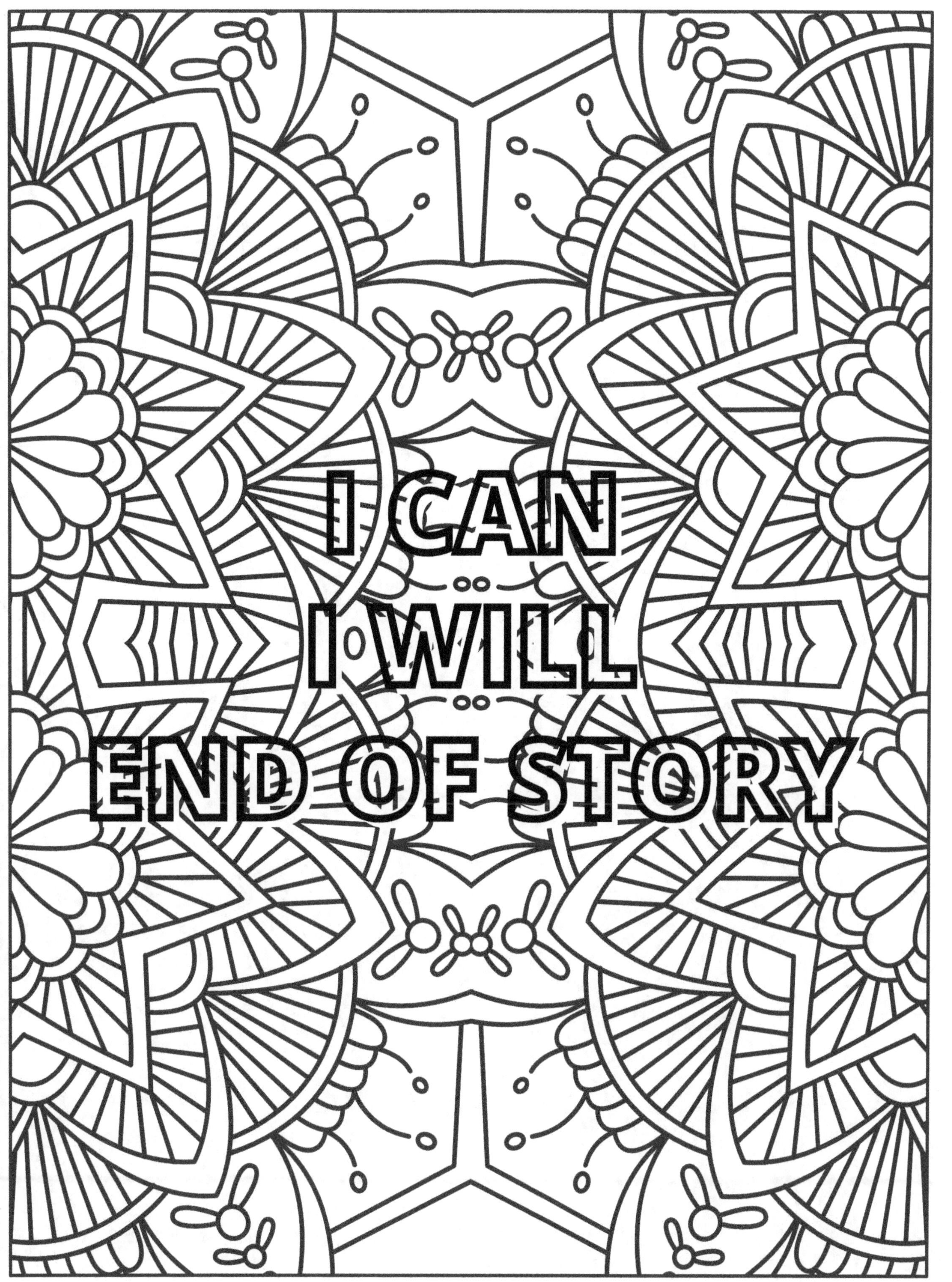

I CAN
I WILL
END OF STORY

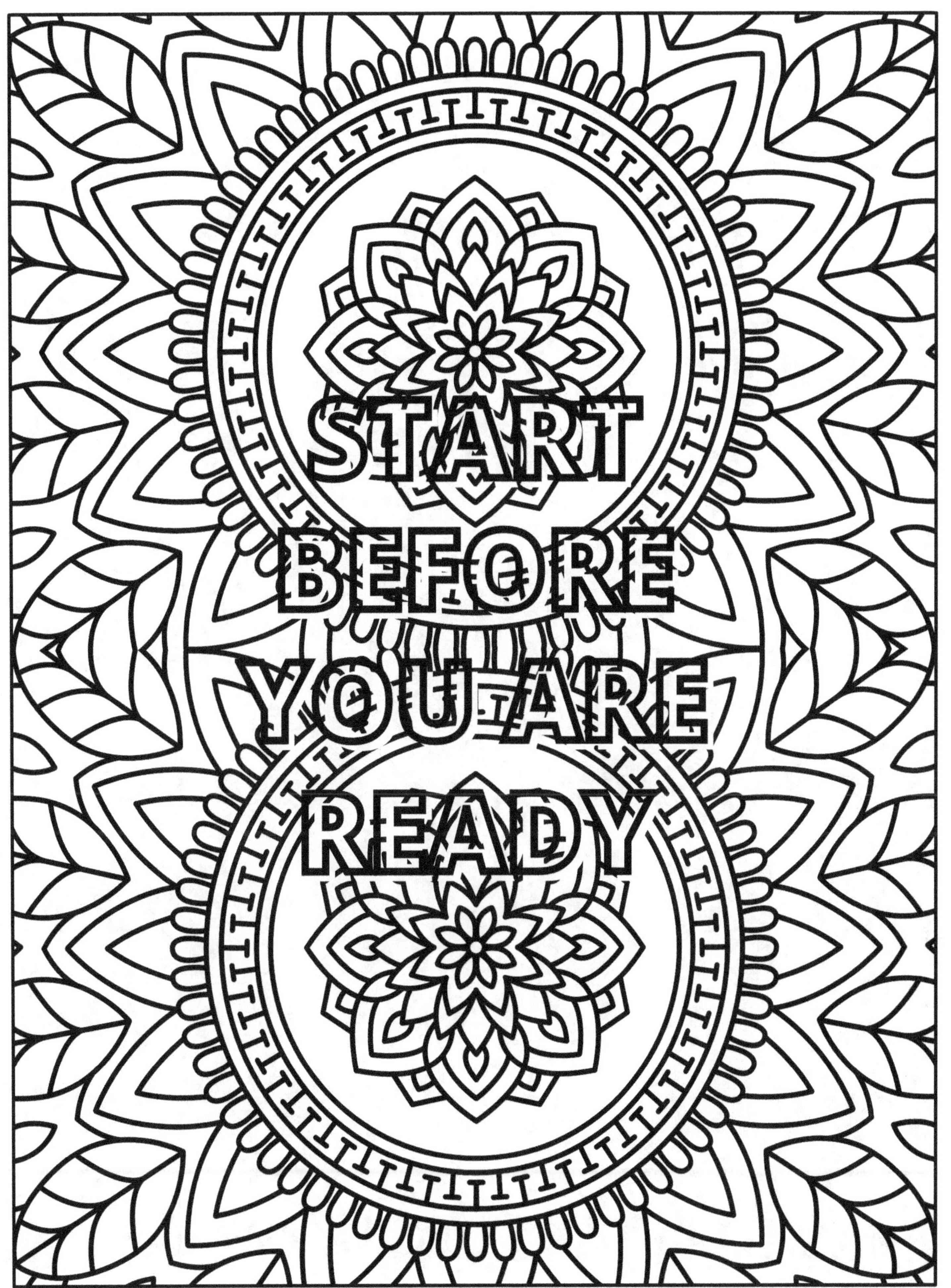

START
BEFORE
YOU ARE
READY

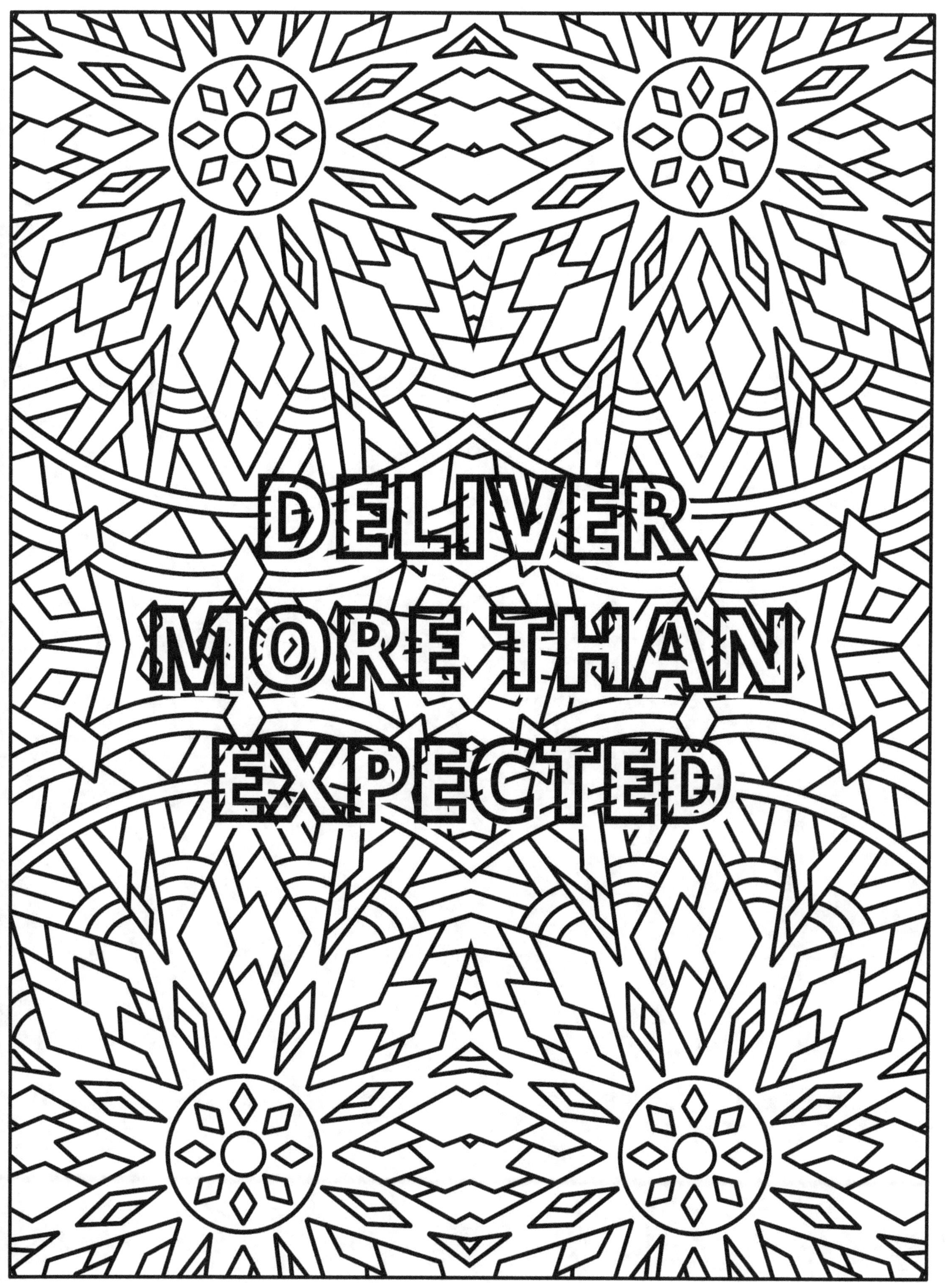

DELIVER
MORE THAN
EXPECTED

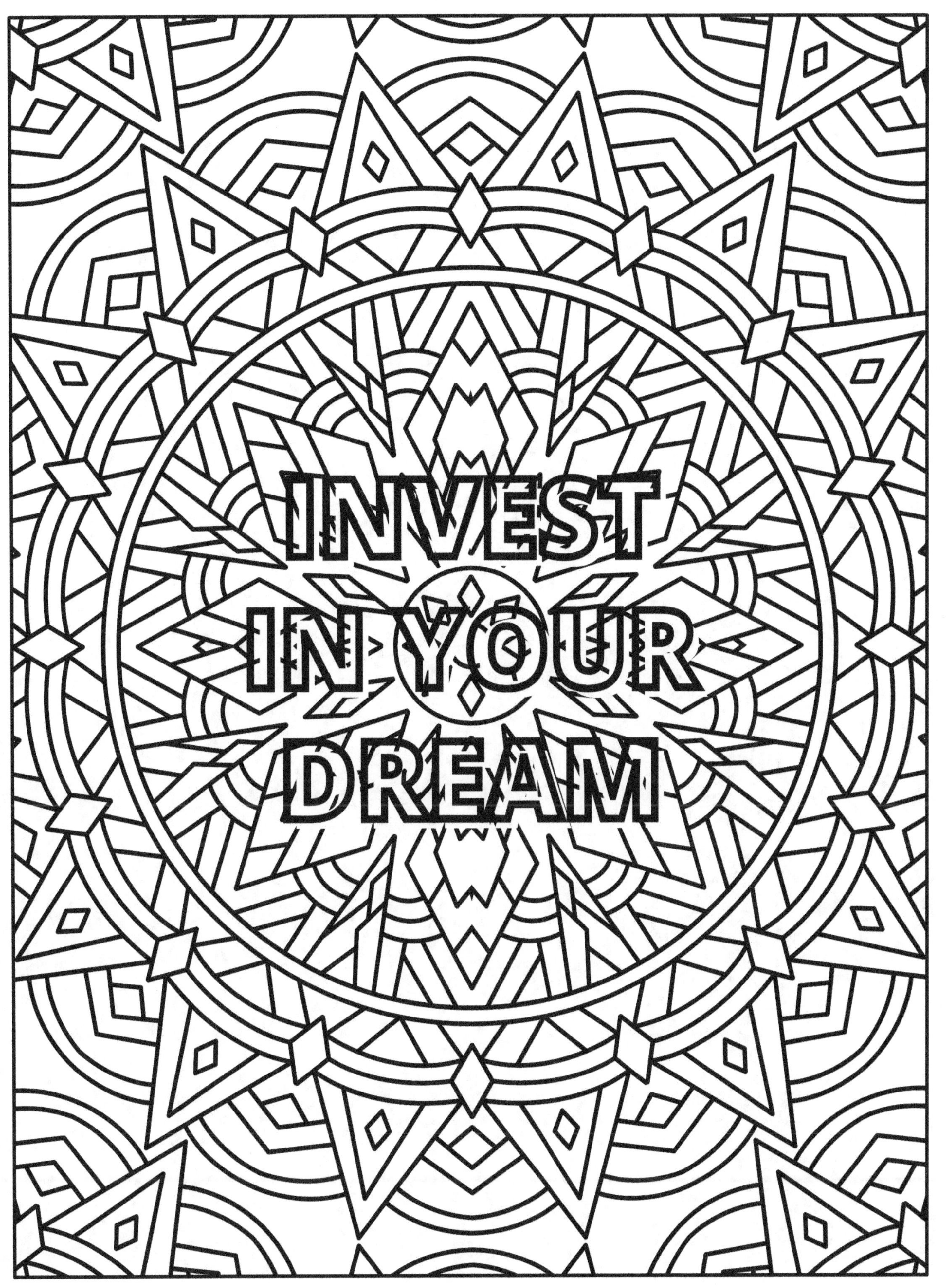

INVEST
IN YOUR
DREAM

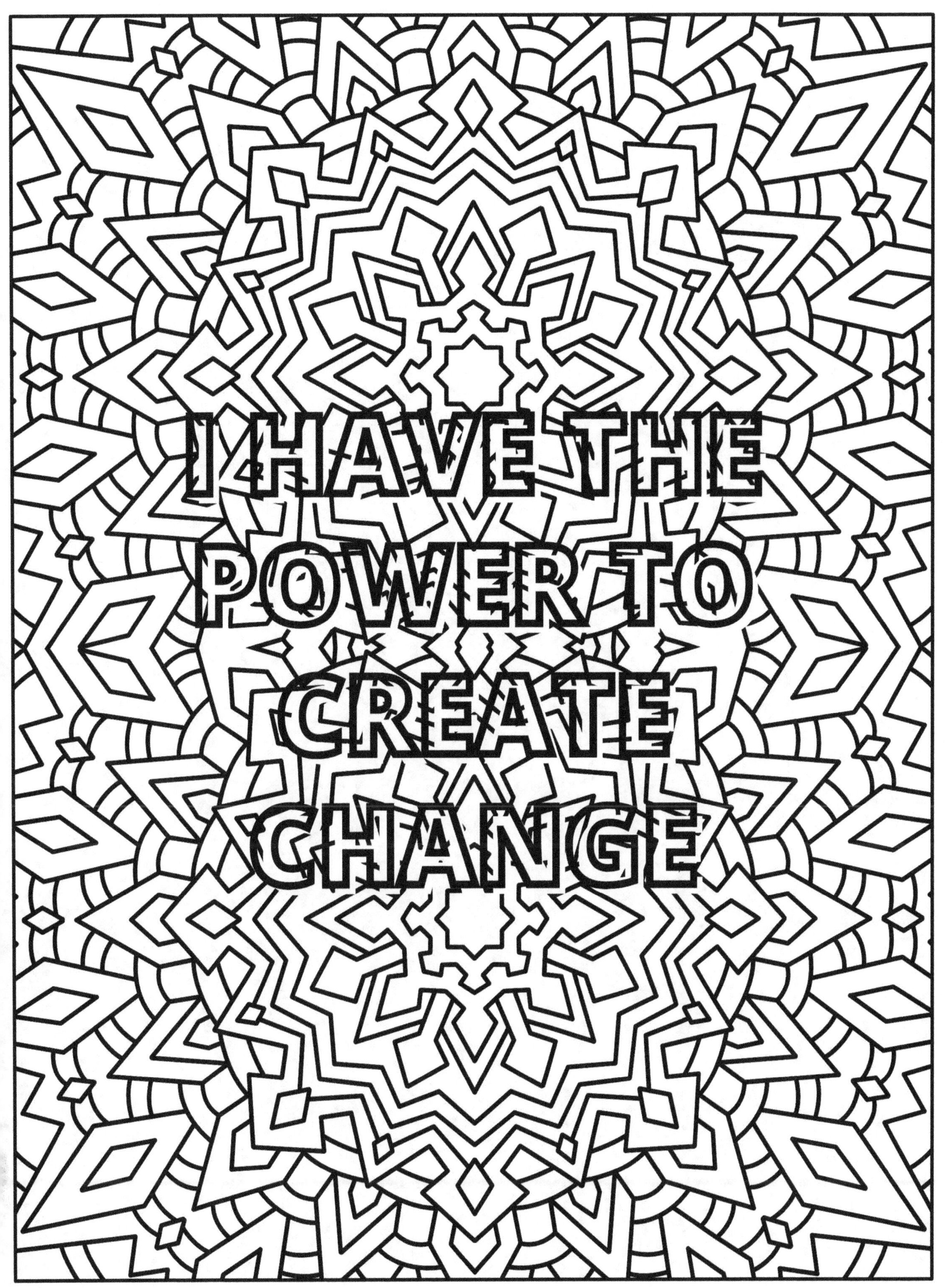

I HAVE THE
POWER TO
CREATE
CHANGE

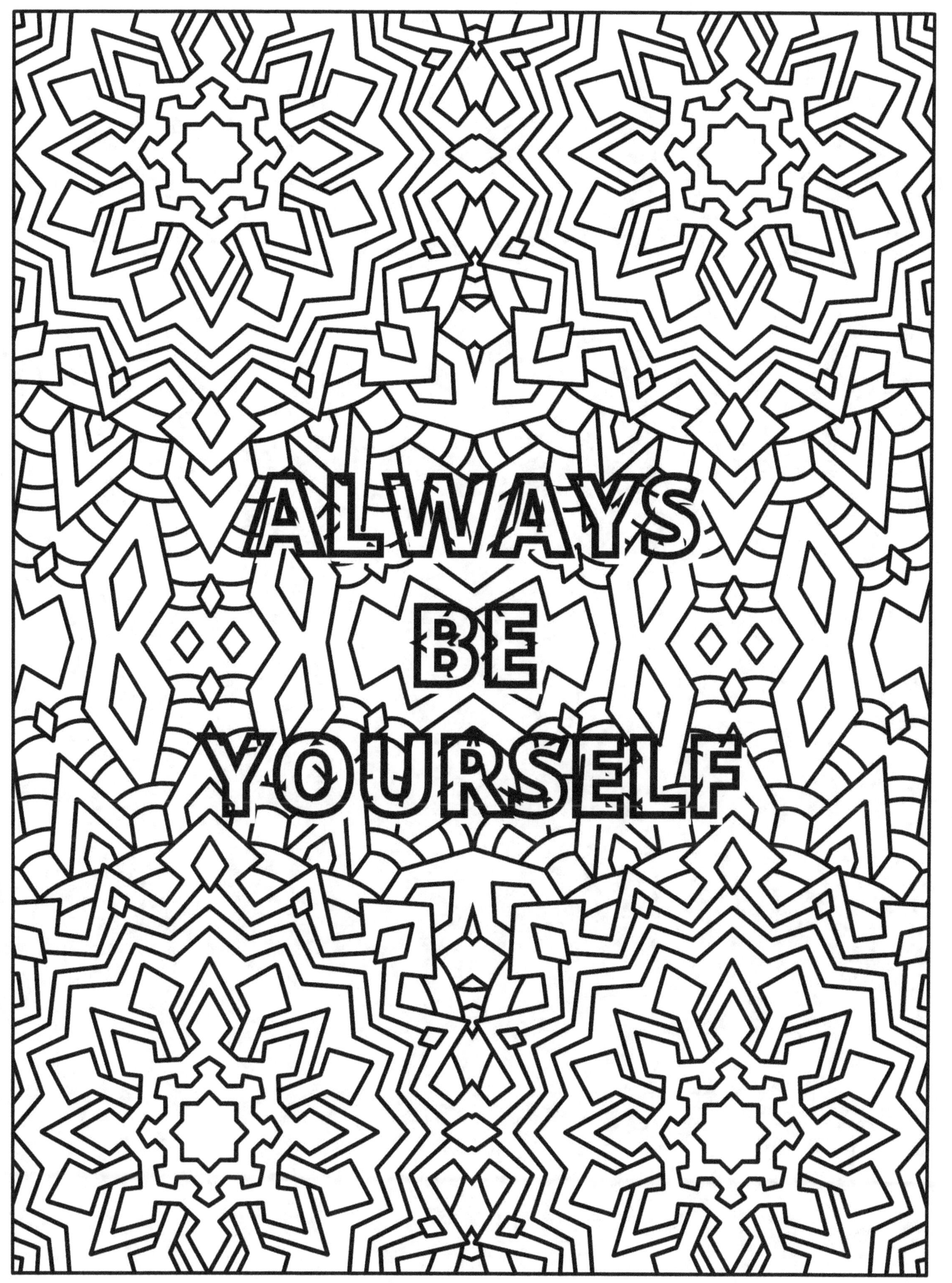

ALWAYS
BE
YOURSELF

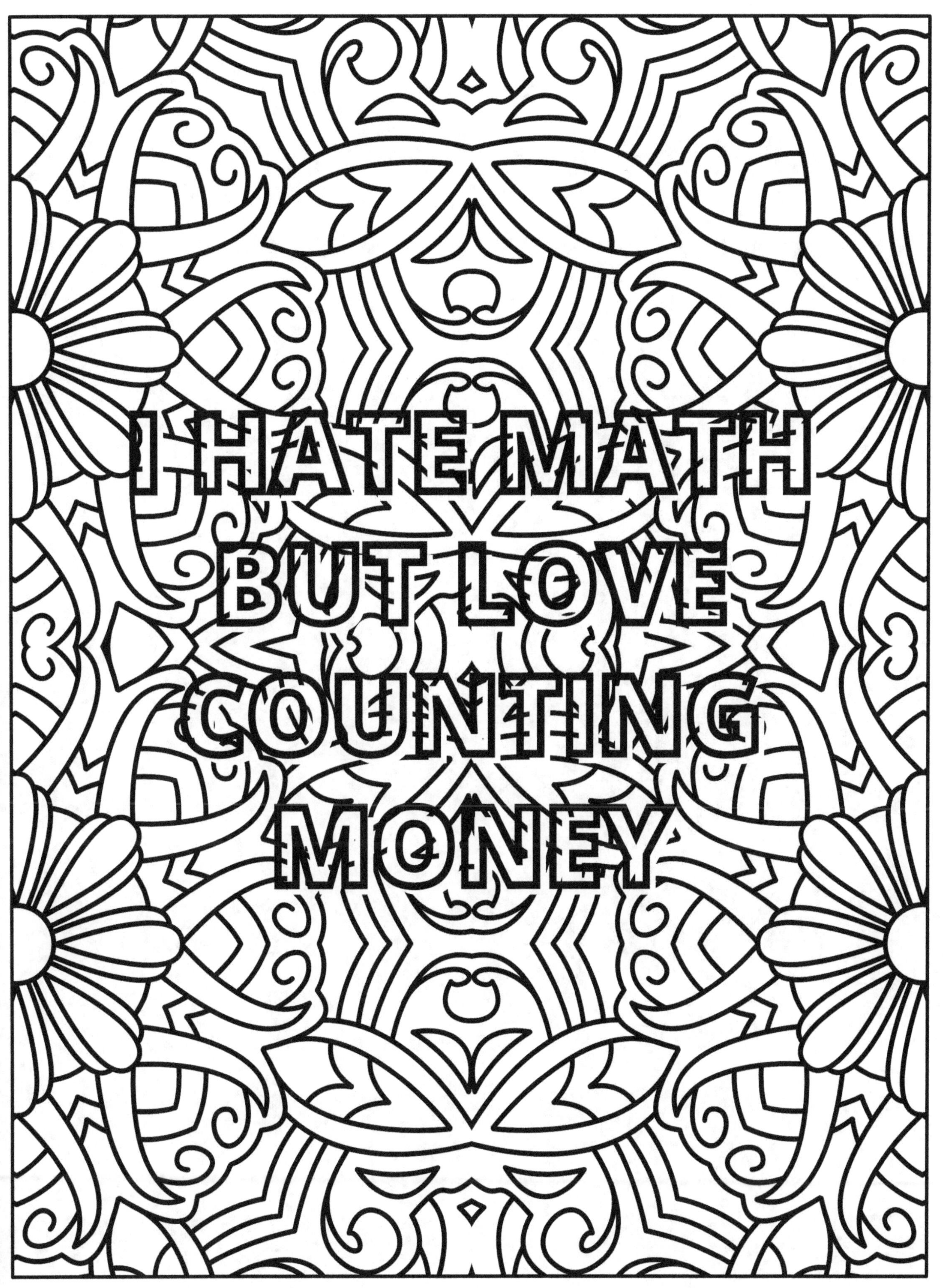

I HATE MATH
BUT LOVE
COUNTING
MONEY

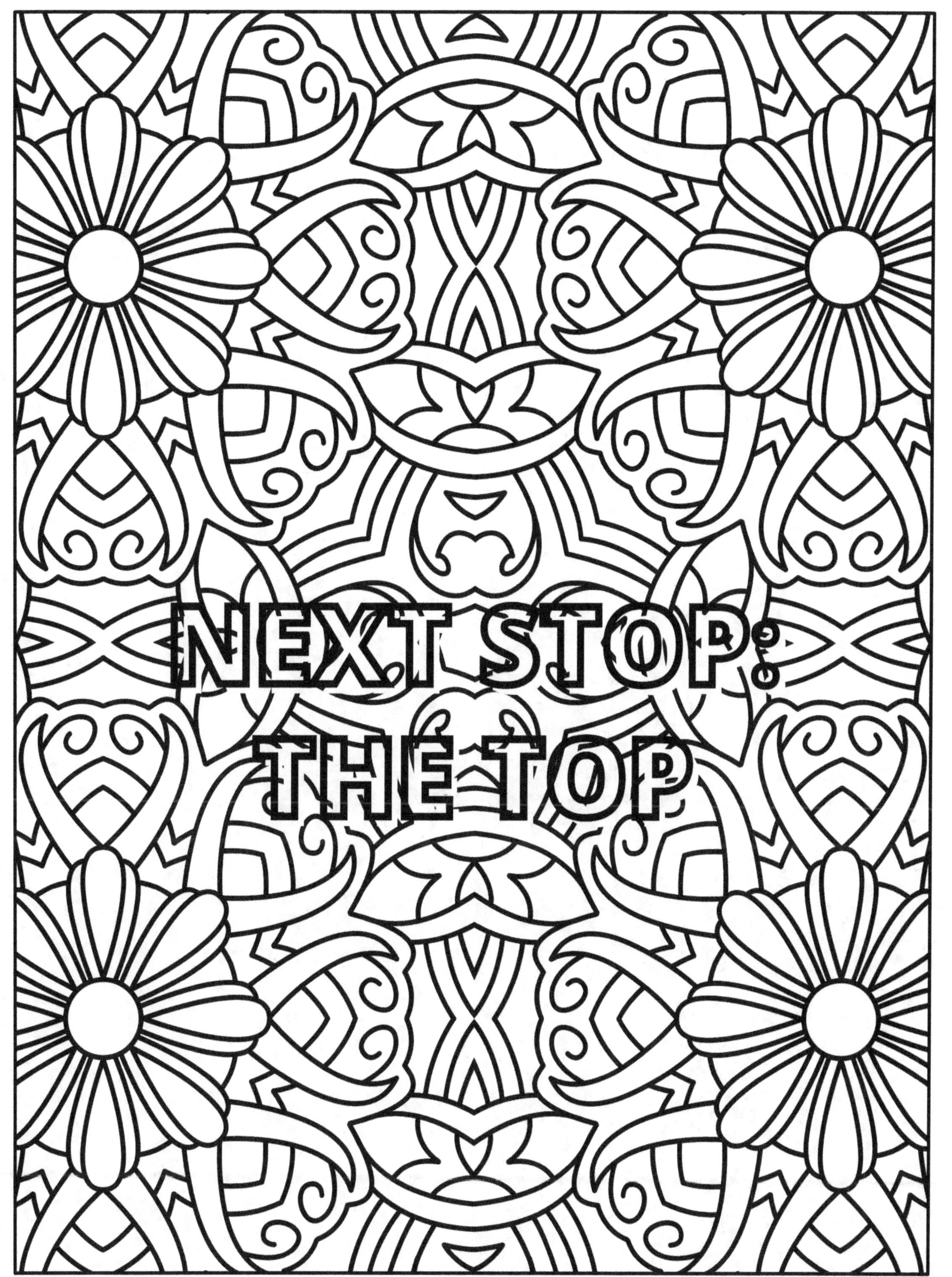

NEXT STOP:
THE TOP

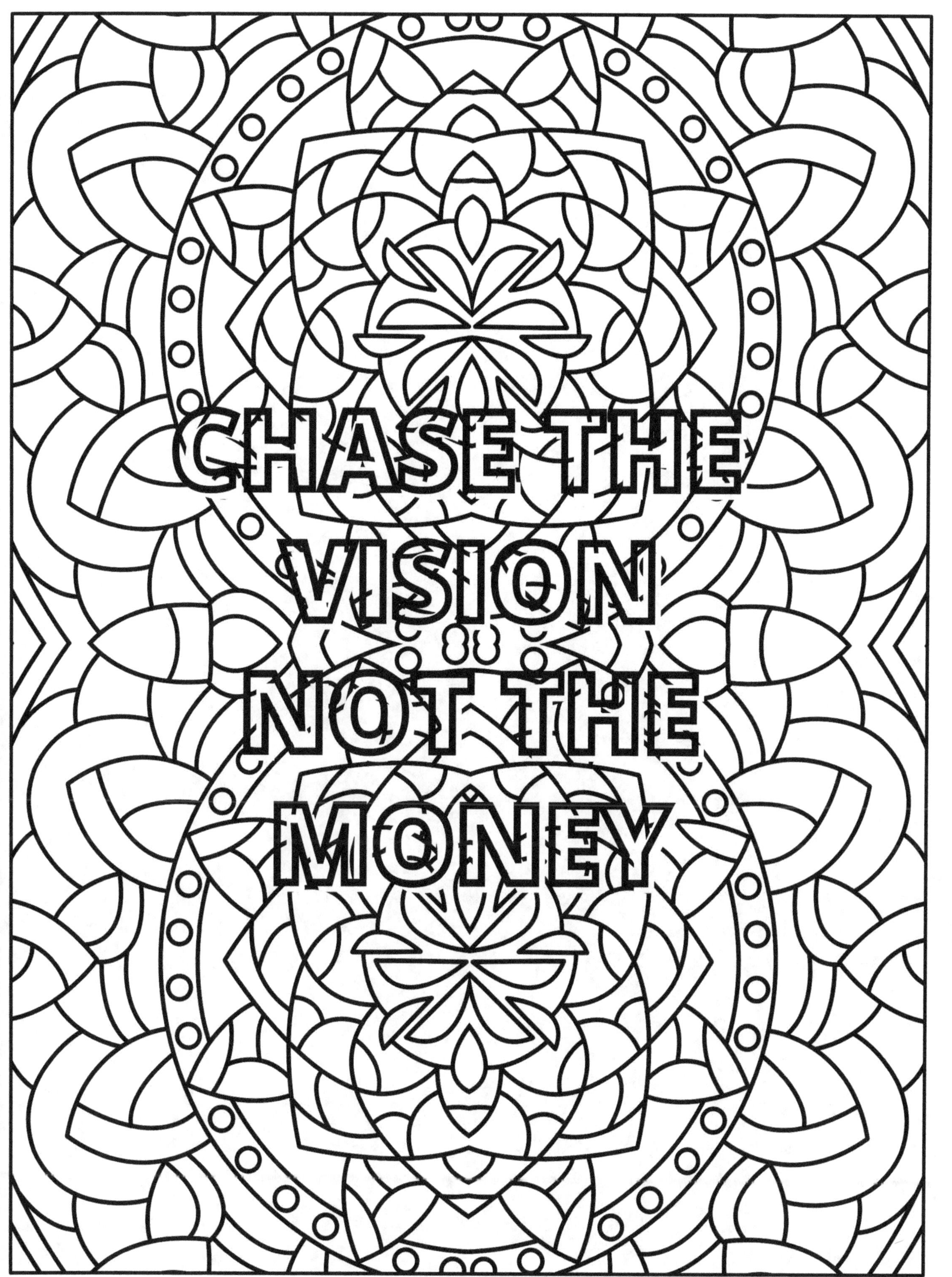

CHASE THE
VISION
NOT THE
MONEY

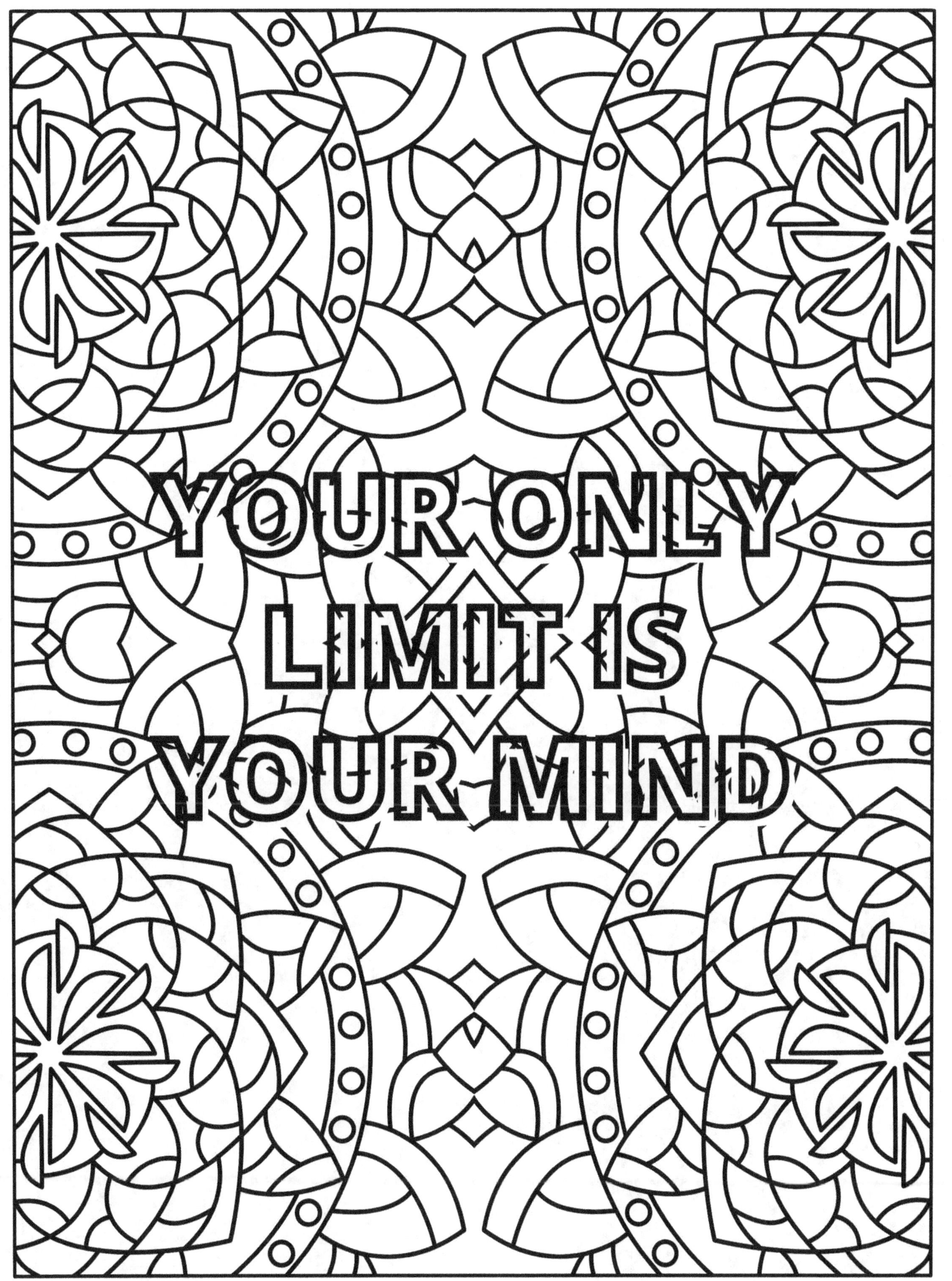
YOUR ONLY
LIMIT IS
YOUR MIND

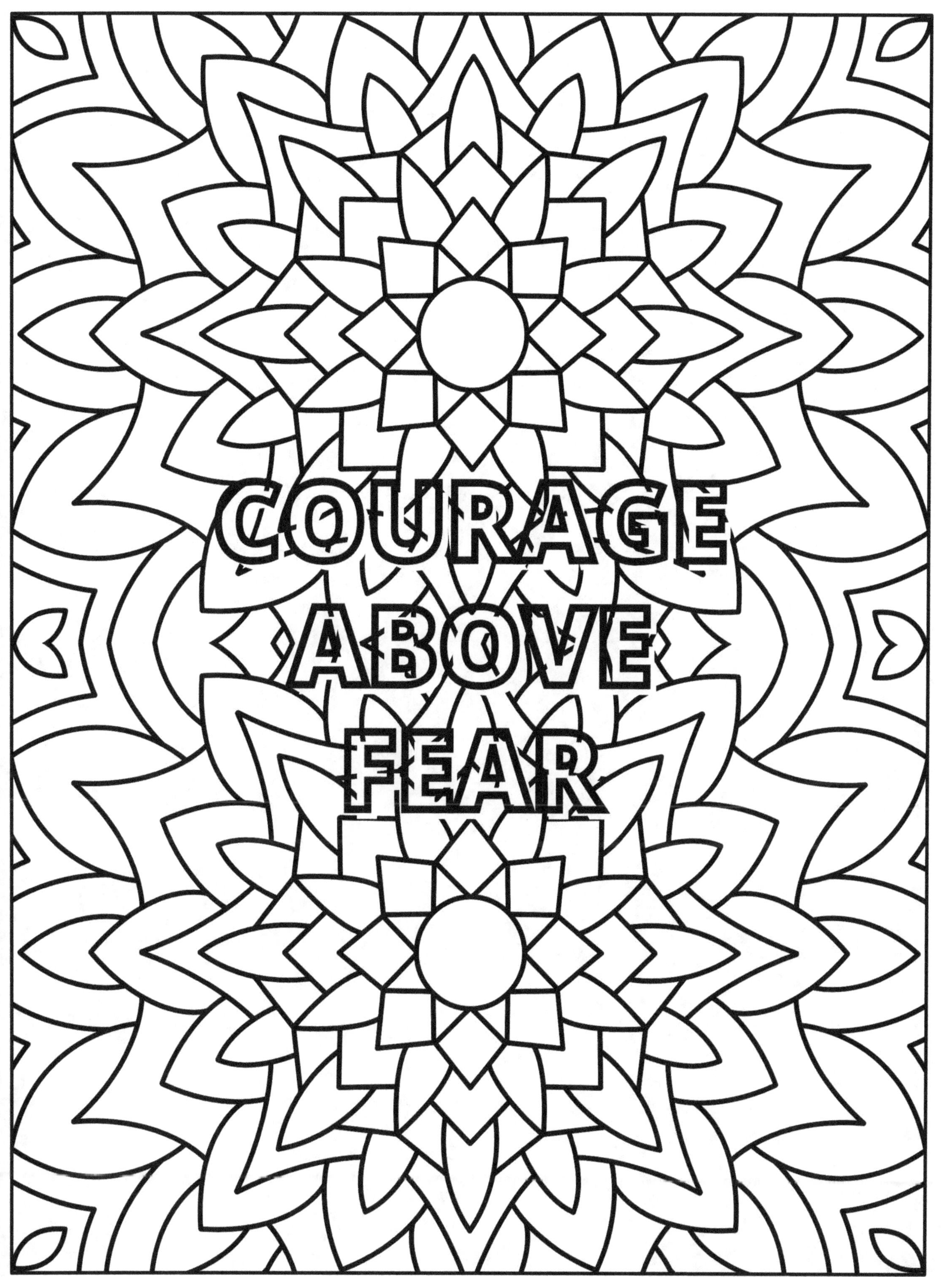

COURAGE
ABOVE
FEAR

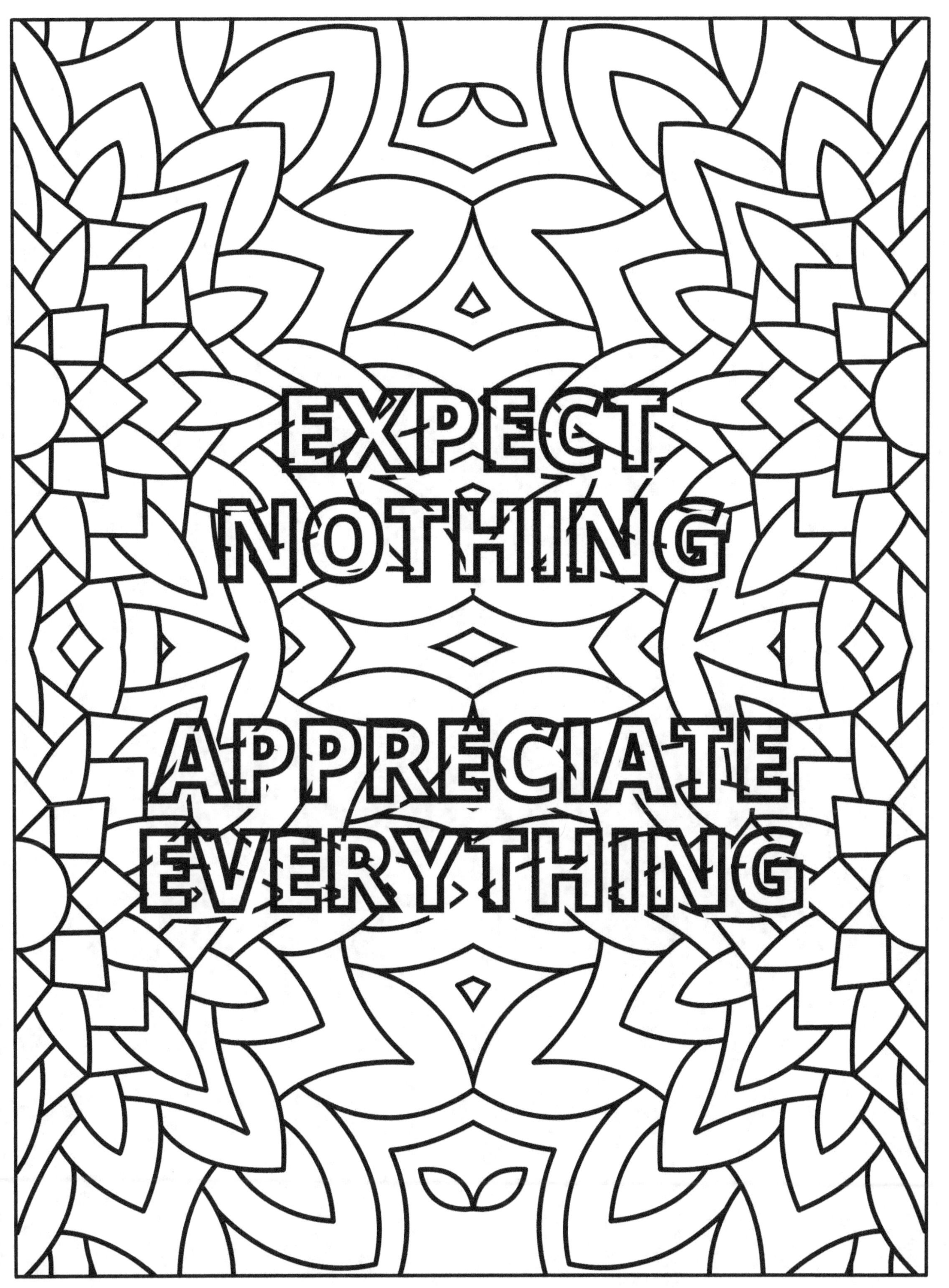

EXPECT
NOTHING

APPRECIATE
EVERYTHING

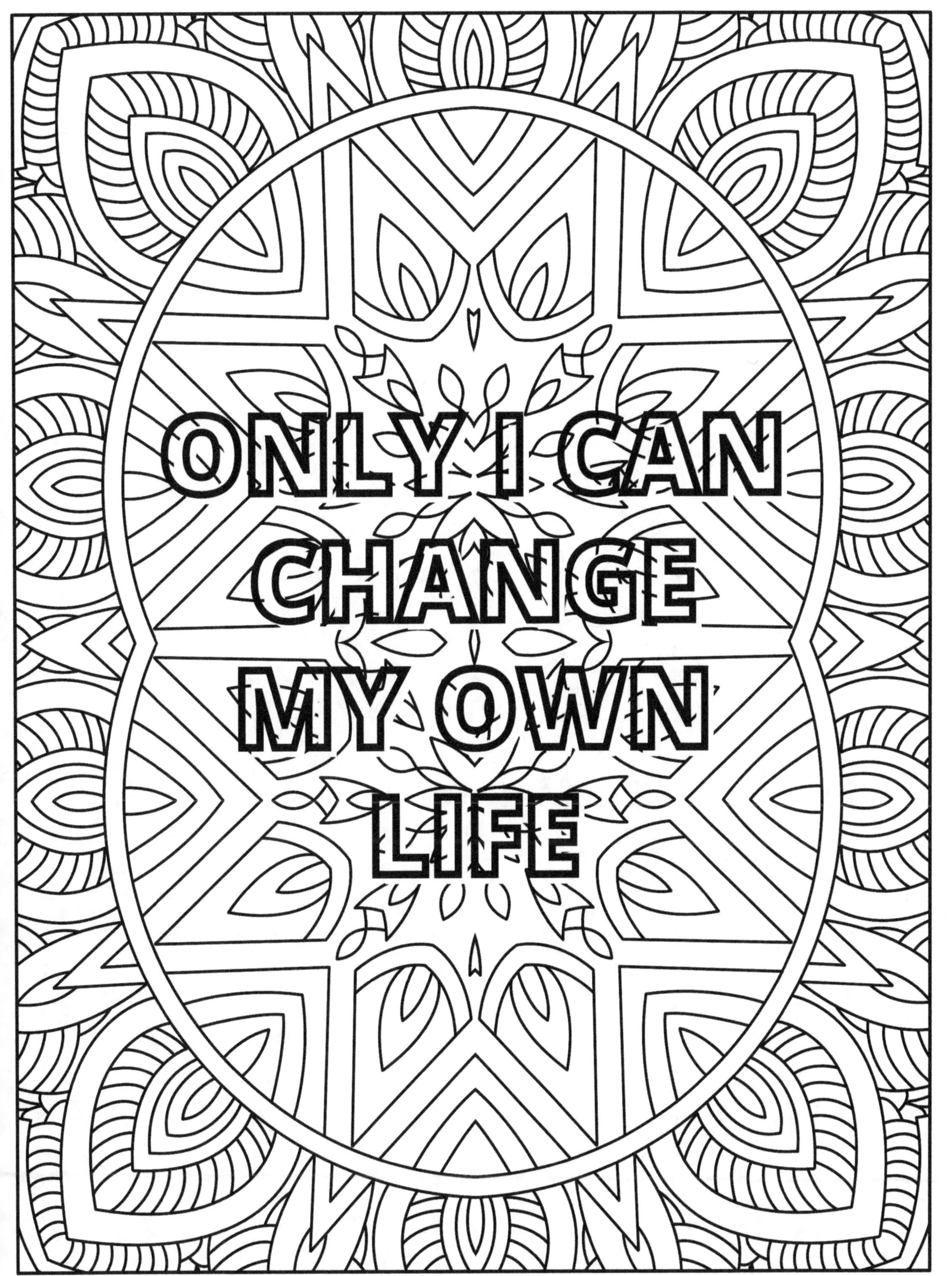

ONLY I CAN
CHANGE
MY OWN
LIFE

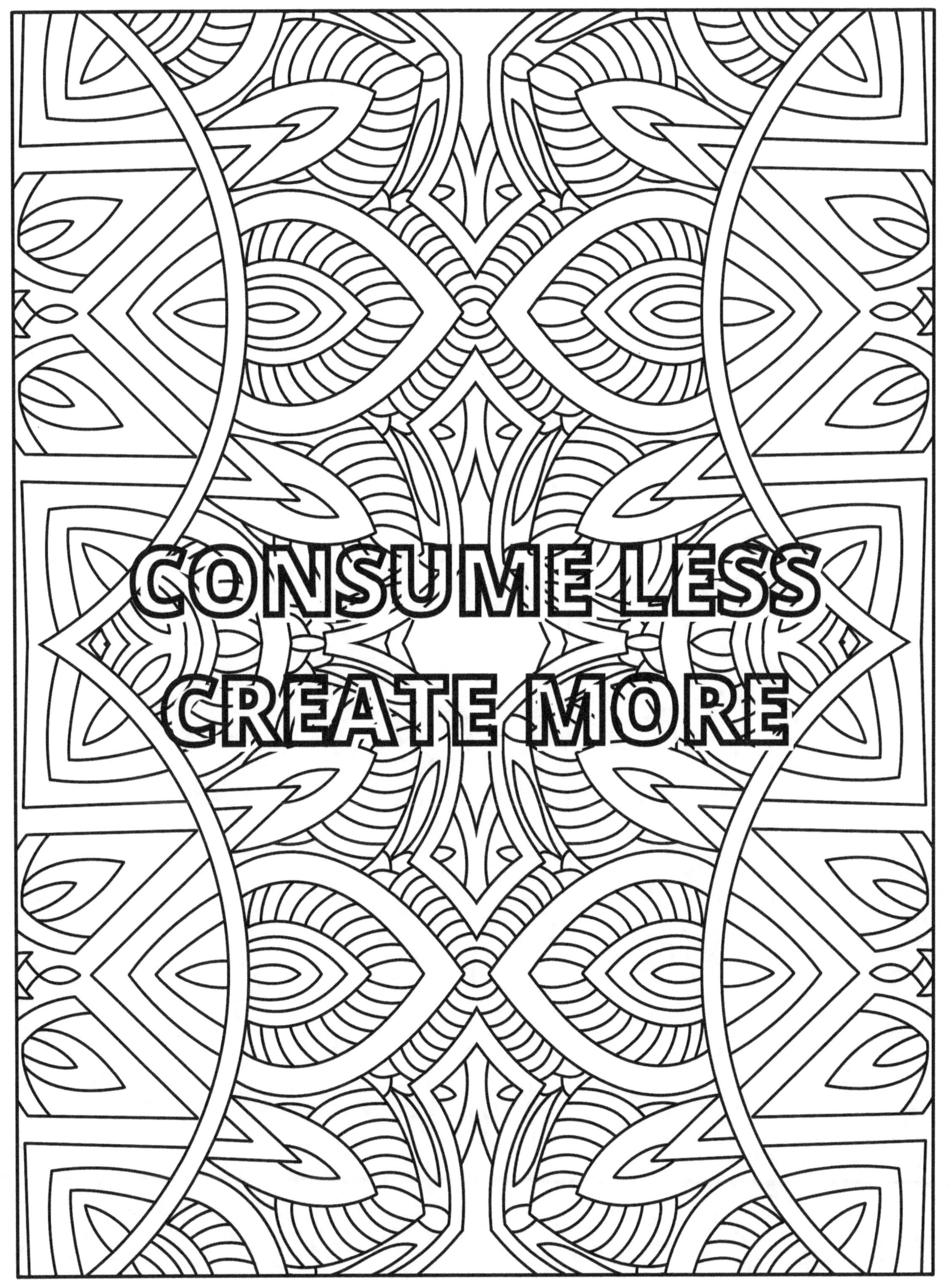

CONSUME LESS
CREATE MORE

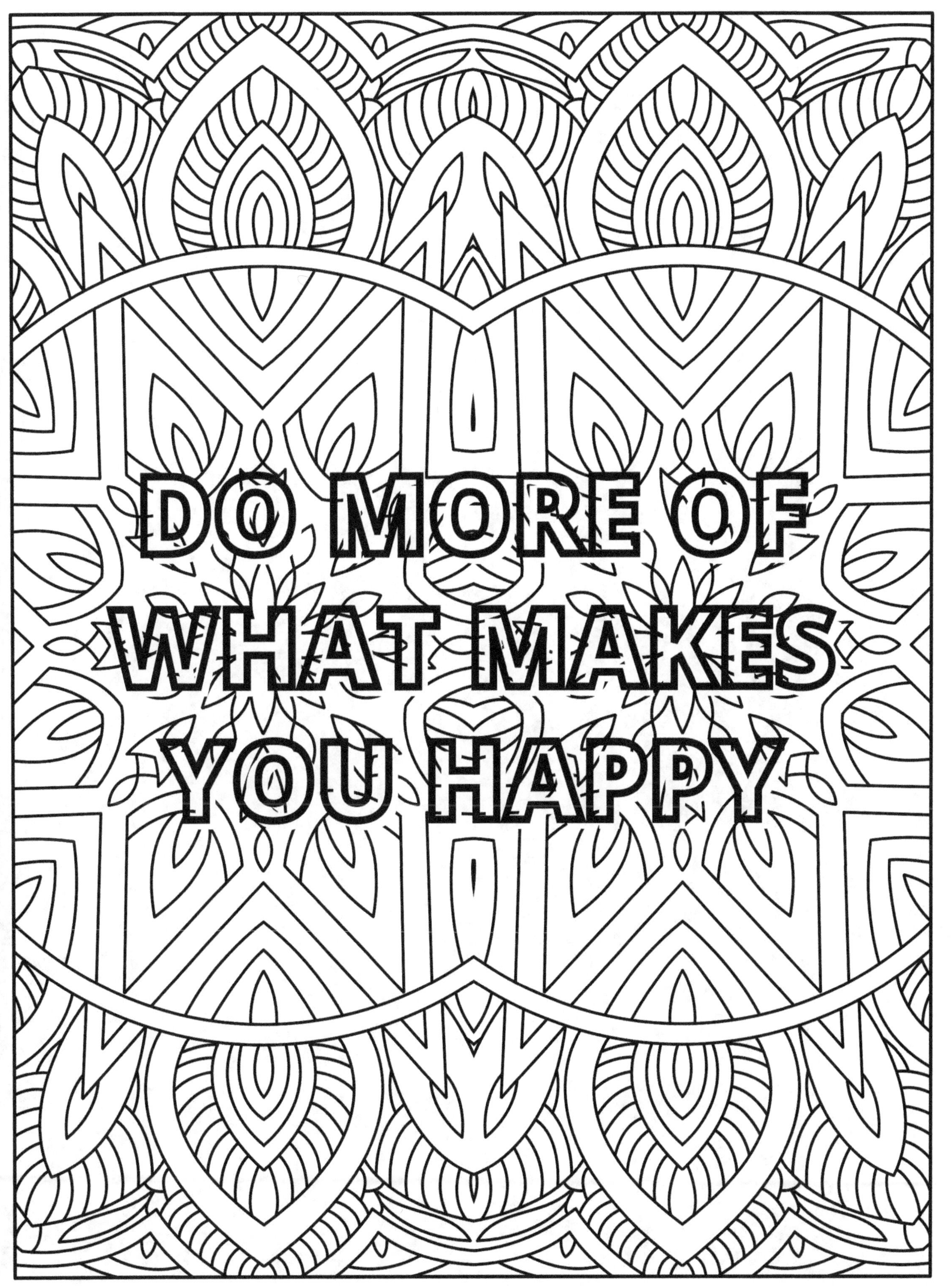
DO MORE OF
WHAT MAKES
YOU HAPPY

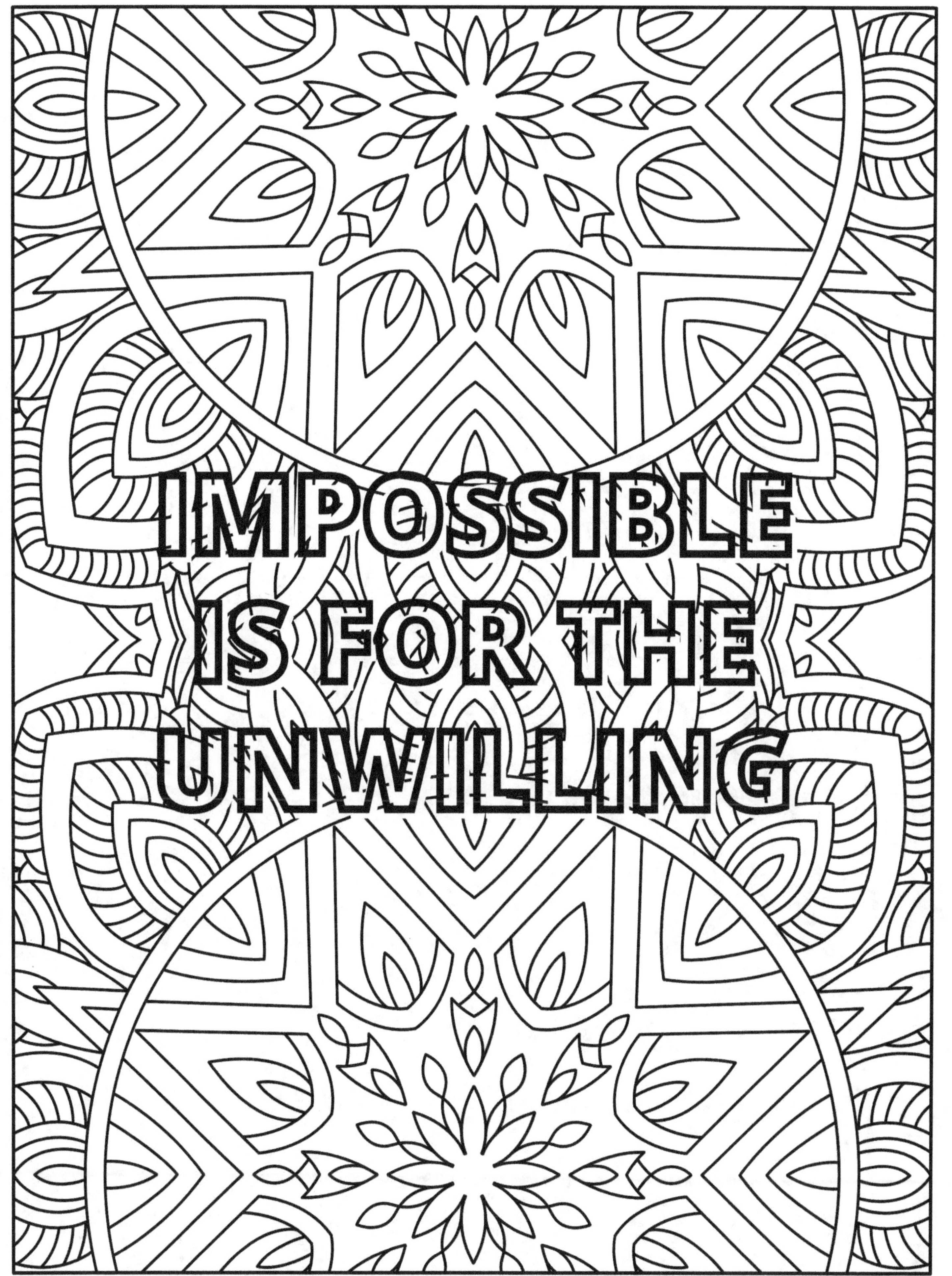

IMPOSSIBLE IS FOR THE UNWILLING

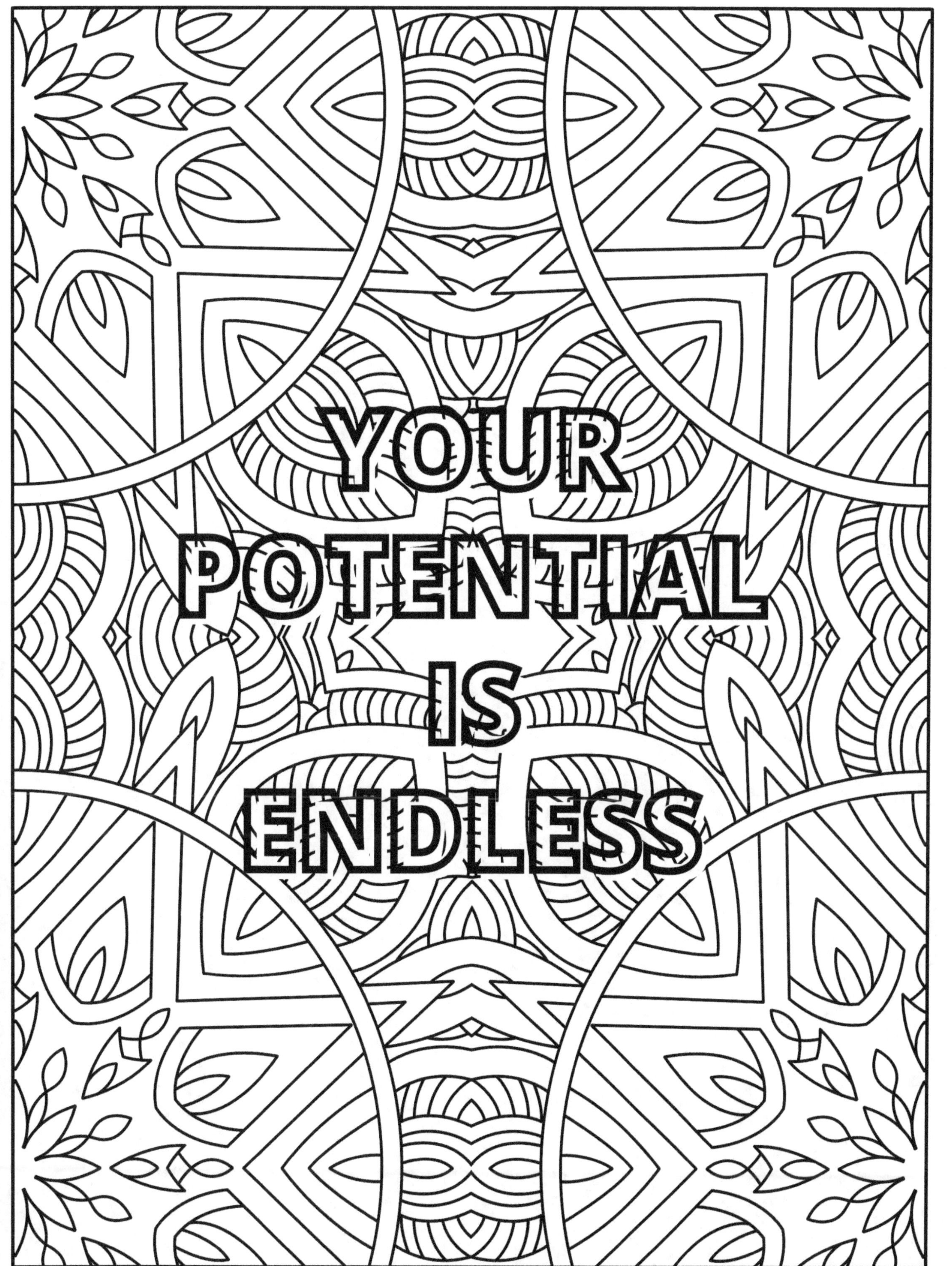
YOUR
POTENTIAL
IS
ENDLESS

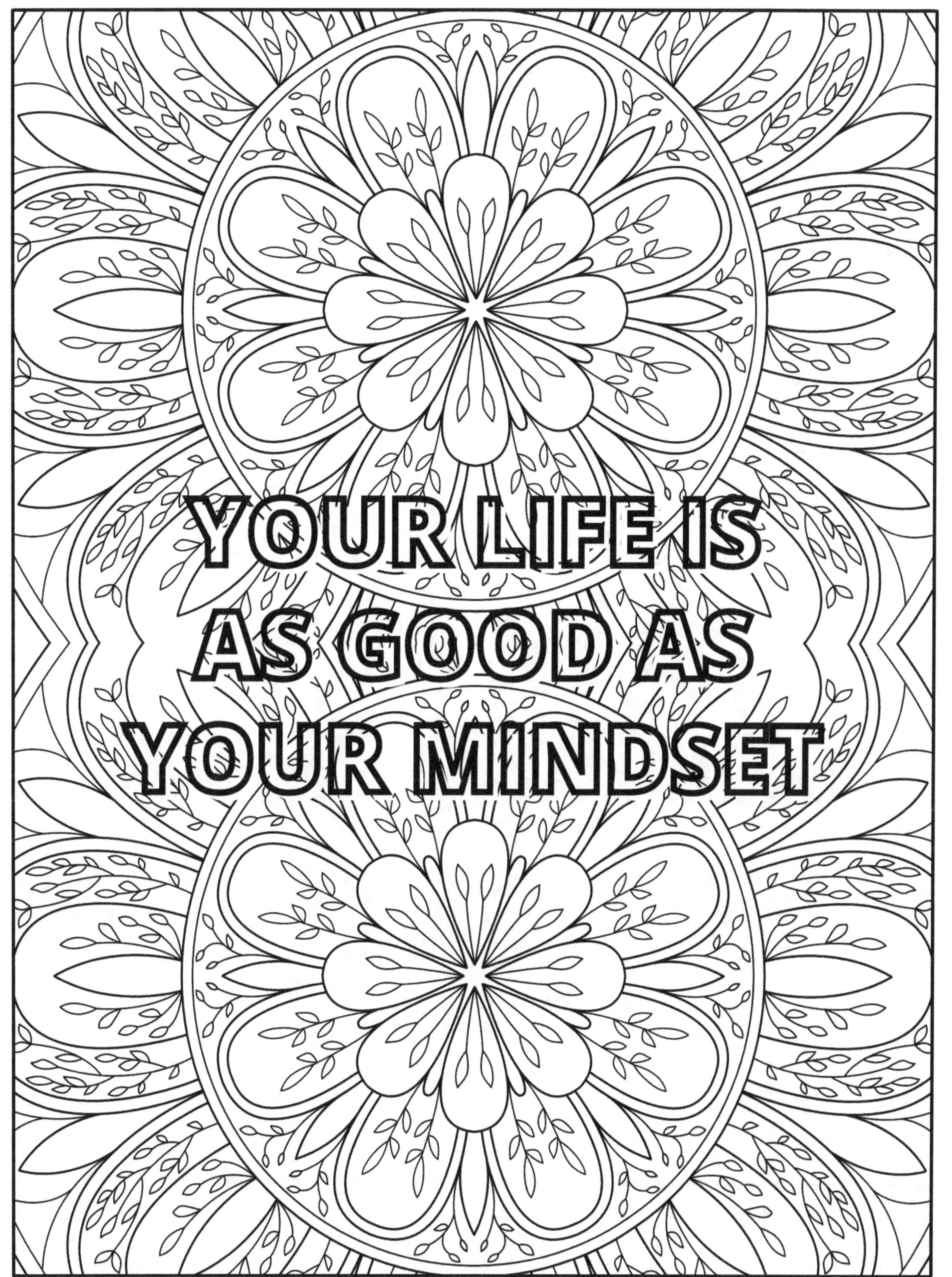

YOUR LIFE IS
AS GOOD AS
YOUR MINDSET

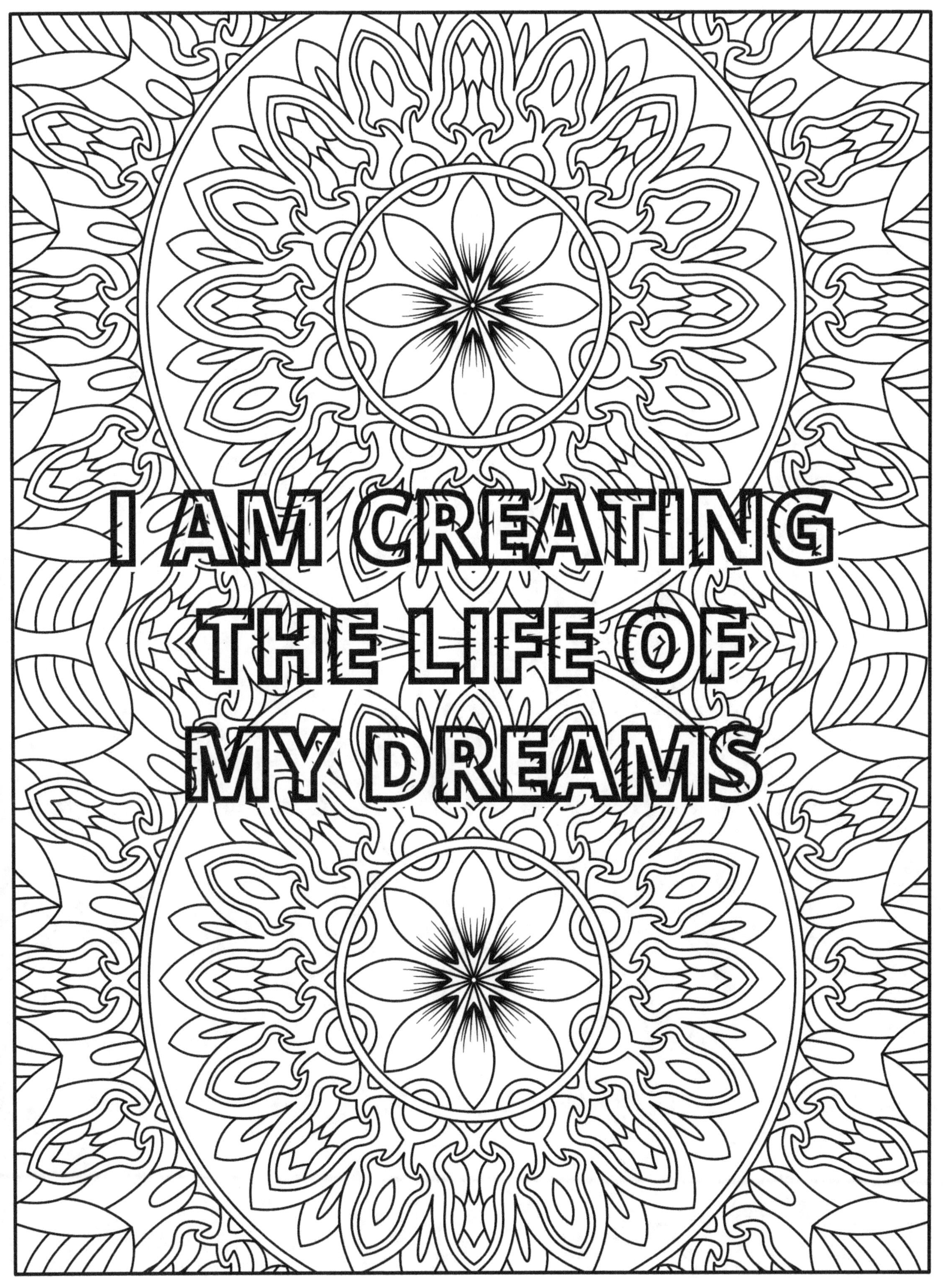

I AM CREATING
THE LIFE OF
MY DREAMS

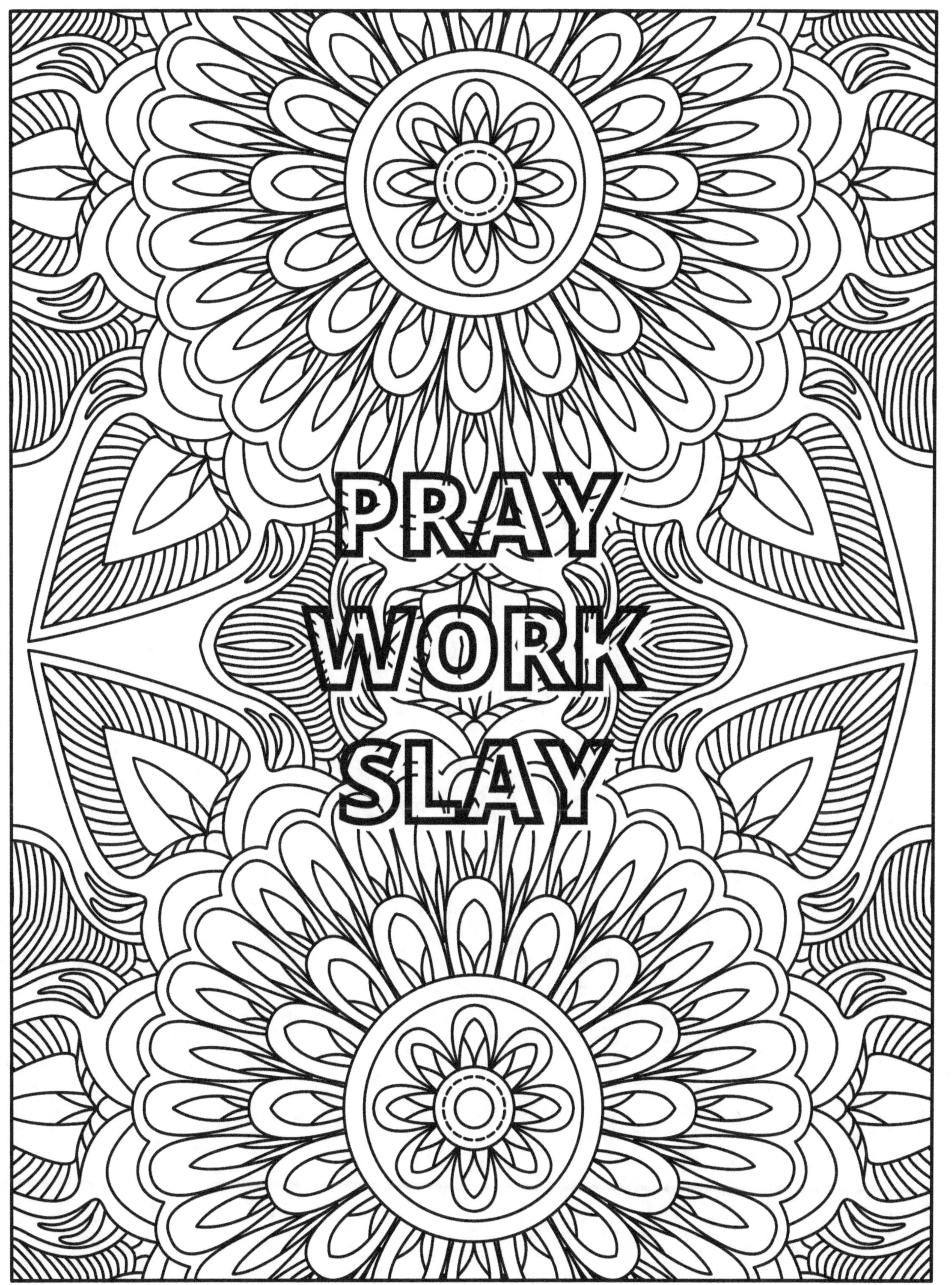

PRAY
WORK
SLAY

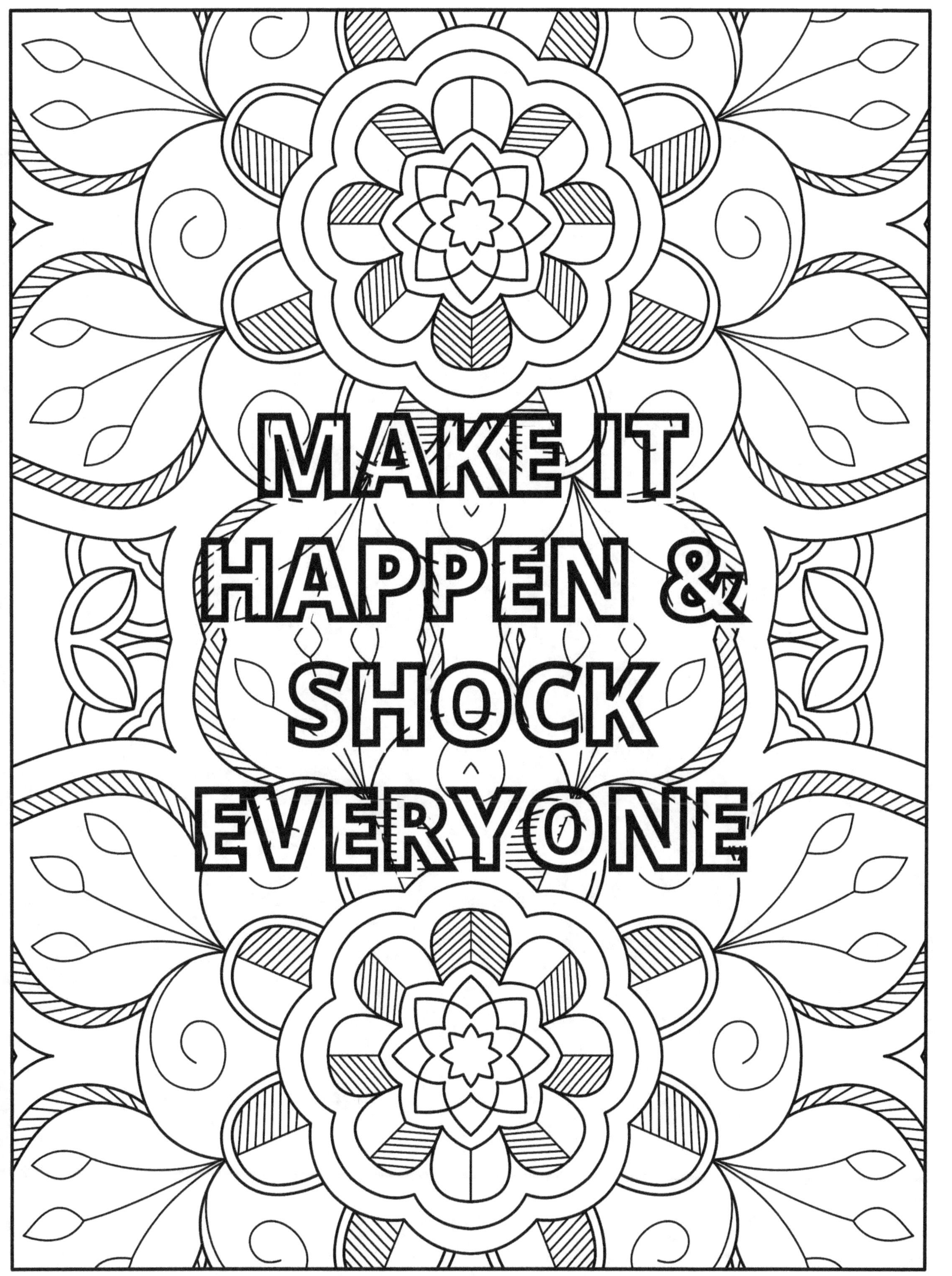

MAKE IT
HAPPEN &
SHOCK
EVERYONE

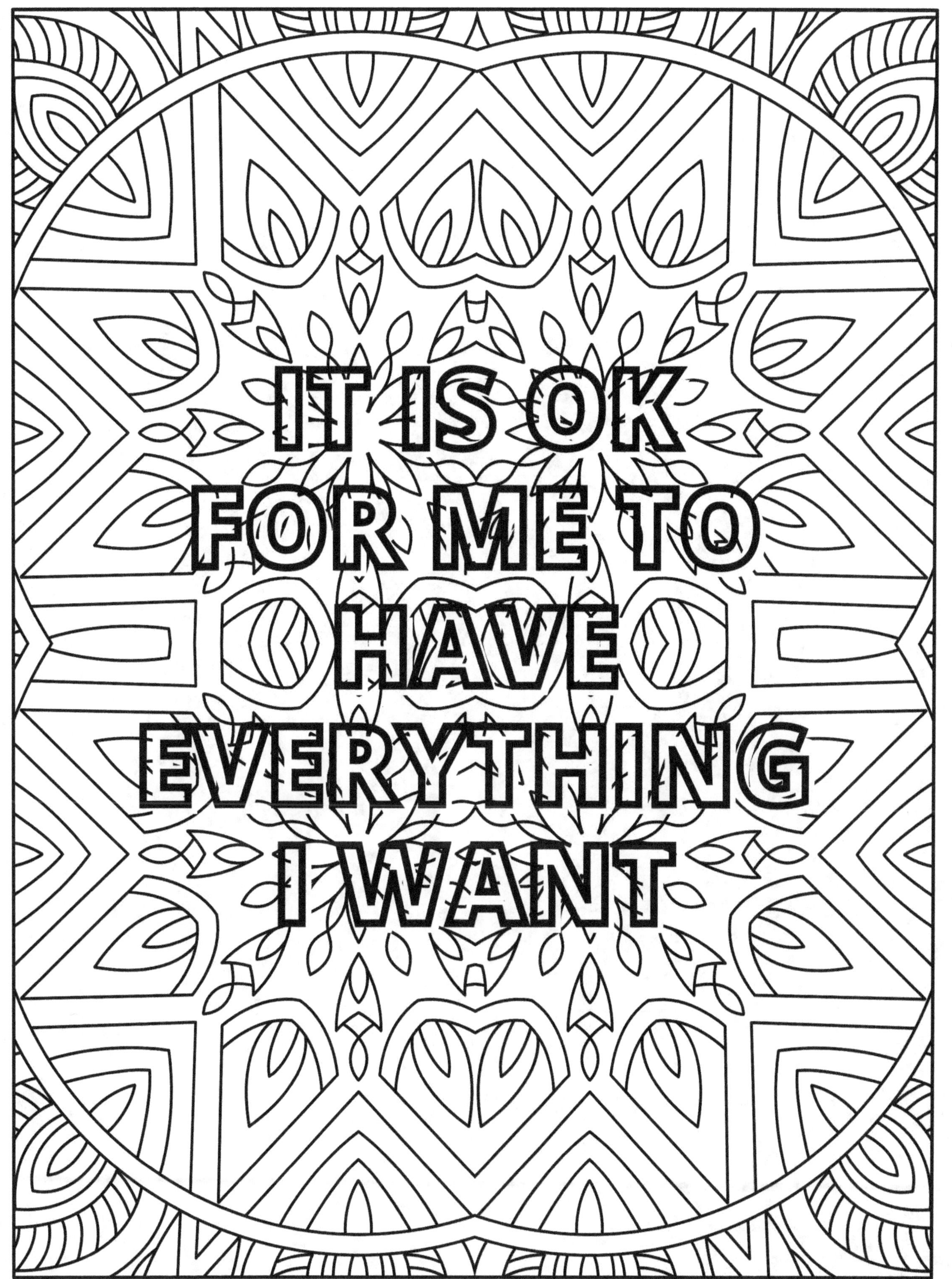

IT IS OK
FOR ME TO
HAVE
EVERYTHING
I WANT